THE CITIZEN'S GUIDE TO POLICE ENCOUNTERS

THE CITIZEN'S GUIDE TO
POLICE ENCOUNTERS

A CONCISE CONSTITUTIONAL HANDBOOK ON
INTERACTING WITH U.S. LAW ENFORCEMENT

LOCHLAINN SEABROOK

Bestselling Author, Award-winning Historian, Acclaimed Artist

Diligently Researched and Generously Illustrated
by the Author for the Elucidation of the Reader

2025

Sea Raven Press, Park County, Wyoming USA

THE CITIZEN'S GUIDE TO POLICE ENCOUNTERS

Published by
Sea Raven Press, LLC, founded 1995
Park County, Wyoming, USA
SeaRavenPress.com

PRINTING HISTORY
1st SRP paperback edition, 1st printing, December 2025 • ISBN: 978-1-955351-80-5
1st SRP hardcover edition, 1st printing, December 2025 • ISBN: 978-1-955351-81-2

ISBN: 978-1-955351-80-5 (paperback)
Library of Congress Control Number: 2026932713

The Citizen's Guide to Police Encounters: A Concise Constitutional Handbook on Interacting with U.S. Law Enforcement, by Lochlainn Seabrook. Includes an introduction, notes to the reader, illustrations, and a bibliography.

ARTWORK
Front and back cover design and art, book design, layout, font selection, and interior art by Lochlainn Seabrook.
All images, pictures, photos, illustrations, image captions, graphic design, and graphic art copyright © Lochlainn Seabrook.
All images created and/or selected, placed, manipulated, cleaned, colored, and tinted by Lochlainn Seabrook.
Cover image: "Ideal Police Encounter," copyright © Lochlainn Seabrook.
All rights reserved.

All persons who approve of the authority and principles of Colonel Lochlainn Seabrook's literary work, and realize its benefits as a means of reeducating the world about facts left out of mainstream books, are hereby requested to avidly recommend his titles to others and to vigorously cooperate in extending their reach, scope, and influence around the globe.

The views documented in this book concerning police encounters are those of the publisher.

PROUDLY WRITTEN, DESIGNED, AND PUBLISHED IN THE UNITED STATES OF AMERICA.

KNOWLEDGE ★ PROTECTS ★ EVERYONE

DEDICATION

To the men and women of law enforcement: You do a job few fully understand, and even fewer could perform. May this book help clarify and strengthen the relationship between officers and citizens alike.

EPIGRAPH

"Police are citizens serving citizens. Society functions most efficiently when both understand they are partners not opponents."

Lochlainn Seabrook, 2025

CONTENTS

NOTES TO THE READER

SOURCES & FOUNDATIONS
☛ This guide is built on established constitutional principles, landmark judicial decisions, statutory frameworks, and long-standing law-enforcement practices. My goal throughout is clarity, accuracy, and objectivity. The information in these pages has been drawn solely from reputable, verifiable legal authorities and accepted training standards.

ABOUT LEGAL INTERPRETATION
☛ American constitutional law is a living system shaped by courts, legislatures, individual states' rights, and ever-evolving professional standards. Because different jurisdictions may apply rules differently—and because case law is continually refined—reasonable disagreements can arise among experts. Where interpretations vary, I rely on the strongest, most widely recognized principles and note when legal standards depend on context, location, or judicial precedent.

LIMITS OF SCOPE
☛ This book explains what citizens and officers are generally allowed to do during encounters. However, it is not a substitute for legal representation, police training, or local statutes. Procedures and terminology differ across states, agencies, and departments. For these reasons, all guidance in these pages should be understood as a broad, constitutionally grounded overview rather than a state-specific manual. I strongly encourage my readers to perform their own individual state-by-state research, particularly when it comes to difficult or complex situations.

LEGAL DISCLAIMER
☛ This book is a general educational guide to understanding police encounters; it is not legal advice and does not replace an attorney. Laws and legal standards vary by state and situation, and readers should consult qualified counsel for guidance on specific circumstances. The author is not an attorney, and nothing in this book creates an attorney–client relationship. Neither the author nor the publisher offers legal advice or assumes responsibility for how this material is interpreted or applied, and readers are responsible for verifying current law in their jurisdiction.

ON SCENARIOS & EXAMPLES
☛ Some examples in this work are simplified to demonstrate underlying legal concepts. Real-world encounters vary widely depending on circumstances, behavior, officer discretion, and local law. Illustrations are designed to highlight key concepts—not to portray exact, universal outcomes in every situation.

ILLUSTRATIONS DISCLAIMER
☛ All human figures depicted in this book are fictional artistic representations created by me solely for educational, entertainment, and illustrative purposes. Any resemblance to real individuals is unintentional.

Introduction

There is a widely acknowledged disconnect between law enforcement and the public. The question surrounds why it exists. Many critics attribute this divide to concerns about police overreach, systemic bias, aggressive tactics, misuse of discretion, improper use of force, and a perceived pattern of misconduct amplified by widely publicized incidents.

My view, however, is that the deeper cause is a widespread lack of understanding of local, state, and federal law. This is paired with a limited awareness of the single document that governs and constrains every police encounter: the Bill of Rights.

In my experience, most police encounters become tense not because the officer intends harm, but because the citizen has no idea what the officer is legally required to do—or what they are legally required to do in return. Confusion breeds fear, and fear quickly transforms an otherwise routine stop into a stressful confrontation. When people do not understand the rules, they assume the worst. When officers encounter that uncertainty they must work twice as hard to maintain safety for everyone involved.

I wrote my book *The Citizen's Guide to Police Encounters* to help bridge this divide. Not by taking sides, not by engaging in political debate, and not by offering commentary on isolated incidents; but by returning to the core principles that govern every police-citizen interaction in the United States: constitutional rights, established case law, and long-standing professional standards. Regardless of one's background, beliefs, or opinions, these fundamental rules apply to all of us equally. As Theodore Roosevelt once said: "No man is above the law, and no man is below it."

My purpose is to make everyday citizens feel prepared, confident, and informed when dealing with law enforcement. By the same token, I want officers to encounter citizens who understand the process, recognize lawful authority, and know what their rights truly are—rather than what internet rumors, television dramas, or ill-informed, and often ill-intentioned, social media activists have taught them. When both sides understand the same rules, encounters become calmer, safer, and far more predictable.

I also hope to dispel the dangerous myths that circulate online—false legal theories, so-called "sovereign citizen" claims, and dramatic misunderstandings of what the U.S. Constitution actually says. These misconceptions have caused untold harm and have led many otherwise law-abiding individuals into unnecessary trouble. Knowledge is not only protection, it is peace.

The material in this guide is intentionally presented in plain English.

You will not find political commentary, moral lectures, or academic jargon. What you will find are the basic legal principles that every citizen should have been taught in school—but rarely was. My goal is not to tell you what to think, but to show you how the process works so that you can navigate any encounter with confidence, composure, and respect.

Many readers have asked why I chose to write this particular book. My lifelong interest in jurisprudence, criminology, nomology, praxeology, penology, and constitutional history all play a part—which is why I have written numerous books on some of these topics.

But there is a more important reason behind this particular work. We are at a critical point in history where, perhaps more than ever, society requires clarity on the subject of the relationship between policing and law: Citizens must know what is expected of them, and officers must know that the people they interact with understand the basic framework of the law. When both sides operate from the same foundation, respect grows naturally. When they do not, distrust flourishes and chaos ensues.

For decades I have watched the steady erosion of basic civics education. Students may graduate with advanced skills, yet remain unable to explain the Fourth Amendment, the difference between reasonable suspicion and probable cause, or the limits of police authority. This gap has real consequences during real encounters with real officers. The Bill of Rights was created for every American, but too few of us know what it says, or even why it was written.

At the same time, policing has grown more complex. Officers must make rapid decisions under pressure while being scrutinized by individuals who often misunderstand the legal standards that govern each action. Sensational headlines, intentionally edited videos, and misleading commentary only deepen the confusion. The weighty burden on law enforcement is extraordinary, and public misunderstanding only makes it heavier.

This guide is not meant to criticize officers or absolve citizens. It is meant to restore a common understanding. If citizens know their lawful rights, they are less likely to panic or escalate. If officers encounter citizens who understand the process, interactions become more controlled and predictable. Mutual knowledge creates mutual confidence, and a confident citizen interacting with a confident officer is far less likely to experience conflict.

Above all, please keep in mind that police encounters are not battles to be won. They are structured legal interactions governed by constitutional rules. When both parties understand those rules, dignity is preserved, rights are respected, and safety is maintained.

Lochlainn Seabrook
Rocky Mountains, USA
December 2025

The Citizen's Guide to Police Encounters

SEA RAVEN PRESS
PARK COUNTY ❦ WYOMING USA
EST. 1995

"Books invite all; they constrain none."
Hartley Burr Alexander (1873-1939)

CHAPTER 1

Why Knowing Your Rights Matters

M ost citizens move through daily life assuming they will never face a police stop. Yet millions of encounters occur every year on roadsides, sidewalks, in public spaces, and even on front porches. In these moments, uncertainty—far more than wrongdoing—is often the greatest source of stress.

A simple misunderstanding can escalate when either person misreads the other's role. This book removes that uncertainty. When you know the rules, the encounter becomes predictable, manageable, and safer for both sides. It also helps distinguish routine conduct from investigative action, which reduces confusion in fast-moving situations. Defined expectations support clearer communication and better outcomes. With accurate knowledge, both sides enter the encounter on steady ground.

THE PURPOSE OF A POLICE STOP
Police stops serve one function: to allow officers to investigate a suspected violation of law or address a safety concern. Your role as a citizen is defined by constitutional limits recognized for generations.

These limits protect your dignity and liberty while still permitting officers to carry out legitimate duties. When these two interests—individual rights and lawful policing—are understood, the process becomes far less intimidating.

WHY CLARITY REDUCES ANXIETY
Anxiety rises during police encounters because most people do not know where their rights begin and end. They may not understand what an officer can legally request, what they must provide, or when they may decline a question or a search. This uncertainty

causes hesitation, which can be misinterpreted.

Officers, for their part, work in a high-risk environment and must make quick evaluations about safety. A citizen who understands constitutional boundaries is better prepared to respond calmly and predictably, reducing tension for everyone involved.

THE FRAMEWORK BEHIND YOUR RIGHTS

Your rights during a police stop arise from the U.S. Constitution:

- The Fourth Amendment protects against unreasonable searches and seizures.
- The Fifth Amendment secures the right to remain silent and avoid self-incrimination.
- The Sixth Amendment guarantees access to legal counsel once formal charges begin.

Together, these amendments form the foundation for every encounter. They establish what officers may lawfully request, what you are free to decline, and when additional protections apply. These protections are reinforced by judicial rulings, including Terry v. Ohio, which authorizes officers to briefly detain someone when they have reasonable suspicion—i.e., a specific, fact-based belief that criminal activity may be occurring.

Reasonable suspicion sits below probable cause, yet must rest on identifiable observations, not speculation. Understanding this helps citizens see why certain limited actions are allowed during a stop, while more intrusive measures require a warrant or a higher legal threshold.

THE REALITY OF LAWFUL AUTHORITY

During a lawful stop, officers may ask for identification, inquire about your presence in a location, or request documentation during a traffic stop. These requests align with recognized safety needs. Officers may control the immediate environment long enough to complete their task safely.

However, their authority is not unlimited. Without probable cause or consent, they cannot conduct full searches, extend a stop indefinitely, or compel answers to investigative questions. Knowing these boundaries helps you respond confidently without appearing confrontational. Awareness reduces misunderstandings in fast-moving encounters.

YOUR ROLE AS A CITIZEN

Your responsibility is simpler than most assume. You are expected to follow lawful commands, present required identification when legally obligated, and avoid actions that may appear threatening. You are not required to volunteer information, debate the officer, or consent to a search. You retain the right to remain silent and may express that right at any time.

A calm, steady demeanor is the most effective way to exercise your rights. It shows cooperation within lawful limits and keeps the encounter stable. Even small choices—such as stating your intentions before reaching for a document—help prevent unnecessary concern. Officers rely on clear, predictable behavior during every stop. When your actions match your words, the encounter remains easier for both sides. Keeping your hands visible and limiting movement helps the officer complete the stop safely and efficiently.

BALANCING RIGHTS & SAFETY

Officers must evaluate risk. Citizens must protect their liberties. These priorities do not conflict when both sides understand the rules. Clear communication prevents escalation, and predictable behavior reduces uncertainty. This book is not about winning an argument. It is about understanding how the process works so you can navigate it responsibly. When each person recognizes the limits of their role, tension decreases immediately.

WHAT THIS BOOK WILL PROVIDE

Each chapter explains a specific type of police encounter in plain English. You will learn what officers may and may not do, what you must and must not do, and what choices are available in real time. You will see how procedures unfold and how your responses shape the interaction. The goal is simple: to give you a firm understanding of your rights and show you how to exercise them without increasing risk. With this foundation, you can move through any stop with confidence.

SUMMARY

A police stop does not have to be confusing or unpredictable. When citizens know their rights and officers follow established procedures, encounters are safer and far less stressful. This chapter lays the foundation for the rest of the book, where each situation will be broken down into clear, practical steps you can use whenever needed.

Understanding the basic limits of law enforcement authority, as well as your corresponding constitutional protections, helps keep everyday police-citizen encounters predictable, calm, and legally grounded. Illustration copyright © Lochlainn Seabrook.

CHAPTER 2

The Constitutional Foundations

Every police encounter rests on a framework older than modern law enforcement itself. The U.S. Constitution sets the rules that define what officers may do, what citizens may decline, and how both sides must conduct themselves. Understanding these foundations provides the structure needed to navigate any stop with confidence. When you know the starting point the rest of the process becomes far easier to understand.

It also clarifies why certain steps occur in a set order and why officers follow specific safety protocols. These guidelines protect both the public and the officer, reducing uncertainty during fast-paced decisions. With this groundwork in place, you can assess each moment of the encounter with clarity.

THE BILL OF RIGHTS AS THE ANCHOR
The first ten amendments, known as the Bill of Rights (ratified in 1791), outline the core protections that shape every police interaction. *These amendments were designed to limit government power and preserve individual liberty.* They do not grant privileges—they recognize rights that already exist and place clear boundaries on how those rights can be intruded upon.

Officers operate within these boundaries whenever they detain, question, sea0rch, or arrest someone. Citizens, in turn, rely on these amendments to ensure that the government's authority remains lawful and proportionate. This structure guides everything from brief encounters to more serious investigative steps. Each amendment acts as a checkpoint that officers must respect. By understanding these limits citizens can identify when an action fits within lawful authority and when it exceeds it.

FOURTH AMENDMENT STANDARDS
Police authority during a stop begins with the Fourth Amendment, which *protects against unreasonable searches and seizures.* To act within this protection, officers must have a lawful basis for the stop. This comes in two primary forms:

1. *Reasonable Suspicion:* A specific, articulable set of facts indicating possible criminal activity. This standard allows brief detention and limited investigation.
2. *Probable Cause:* A higher standard indicating a fair probability that a crime has been committed. This level of justification allows for arrest and full searches.

These standards are not theoretical. They sculpt every moment of a police stop. When an officer detains a driver, requests identification, or examines the immediate area for safety purposes, each action must align with one of these thresholds.

FIFTH AMENDMENT PROTECTIONS

The Fifth Amendment provides *the right to remain silent and protects against compelled self-incrimination.* During a police stop, this means you can decline to answer investigative questions. You may state clearly and politely that you are choosing to remain silent. This right does not interfere with an officer's ability to complete the necessary parts of a stop, however, such as requesting identification or issuing lawful instructions for safety.

The Fifth Amendment also underpins *your right to refuse consent to a search.* Officers may ask for permission to examine your vehicle, your pockets, or your belongings. You may decline. Your refusal cannot be used as evidence of wrongdoing. It simply preserves your constitutional boundary.

SIXTH AMENDMENT GUARANTEES

If a stop progresses into formal arrest and charges, the Sixth Amendment *ensures access to legal counsel.* This right begins once the government initiates prosecution. While *it does not apply during the earliest stages of roadside stops*, it becomes central if the encounter transitions to custodial interrogation or criminal proceedings. Understanding *when* this right activates helps citizens know what to expect after an arrest. It also reinforces the principle that no one must face the power of the state without the assistance of a legal advocate.

THE TERRY RULE

A pivotal part of constitutional policing is the principle established in Terry v. Ohio. This decision permits officers to conduct a brief stop based on reasonable suspicion and to perform a limited pat-down if they reasonably believe a person may be armed. The purpose is officer safety, not evidence gathering.

The pat-down is confined to checking for weapons, not general searching. Citizens benefit from recognizing this boundary, because it clarifies why certain actions occur and why they are not open-ended. It also emphasizes the difference between a quick safety check and a full search, which requires probable cause or consent. Courts have consistently upheld this distinction to prevent routine stops from expanding without justification. By understanding these limits citizens can better interpret an officer's actions in the moment.

WARRANTS & THEIR LIMITS
While many police encounters occur without warrants, the warrant requirement remains a central constitutional safeguard. A warrant must be issued by a neutral authority, based on probable cause, and must describe the specific place or items involved. This requirement prevents general or exploratory searches. For stops that do not involve warrants, the constitutional standards described earlier control the officer's actions. A warrant also confines officers to the scope it describes; they may not exceed its boundaries or search areas not reasonably connected to its terms. If circumstances change, officers must rely on a separate exception or obtain a new warrant. These limits ensure that judicial oversight—not discretion in the moment—guides more intrusive searches.

WHY THESE PRINCIPLES MATTER IN DAILY LIFE
Most citizens will experience police stops in routine settings, such as traffic enforcement or brief investigative encounters, all of which are governed by constitutional structure. When citizens understand the limits on searches, the rules governing questioning, and the standards officers must meet, the encounter becomes far less intimidating. Knowledge replaces uncertainty and supports safer, calmer communication while helping citizens recognize when an officer's request is routine rather than exceptional. This distinction reduces unnecessary tension and prevents misunderstandings so that daily interactions remain predictable and manageable.

SUMMARY
The Constitution forms the backbone of every police stop. The Fourth, Fifth, and Sixth Amendments outline what officers may do and what citizens may decline. Reasonable suspicion, probable cause, warrants, and the Terry rule create predictable boundaries. When these foundations are understood, the entire encounter becomes more manageable and significantly less stressful.

The U.S. Supreme Court helps establish and maintain the constitutional authority that governs all police–citizen encounters. Illustration copyright © Lochlainn Seabrook.

CHAPTER 3

What Police Are Allowed to Do During Encounters

Police encounters follow a defined legal framework. Officers must balance their duty to enforce the law with the constitutional boundaries that protect citizens.

This chapter explains what officers may lawfully do during stops, detentions, and brief investigative encounters, and what limits apply to those actions. The goal is to give you the reader a clear sense of what to expect, so routine interactions stay predictable and safe.

It also shows how each level of contact carries its own standard, from casual questioning to reasonable suspicion to probable cause. Understanding these tiers prevents confusion when an encounter shifts. With this foundation you can recognize the boundaries on both sides and respond with clarity.

AUTHORITY TO INITIATE CONTACT
Officers may begin an encounter in several ways. They may approach voluntarily to ask questions. They may stop an individual briefly if they have reasonable suspicion, a standard based on specific, articulable facts indicating that a law has been or is about to be violated. They may also conduct a full arrest only when they have probable cause; meaning they possess facts strong enough to support a reasonable belief that a crime has occurred.

Understanding these thresholds helps citizens know why an encounter is happening and what level of authority the officer is exercising at that moment. *Voluntary conversation requires no suspicion; an investigative stop requires reasonable suspicion; an arrest requires probable cause.*

REQUESTS FOR IDENTIFICATION & DOCUMENTATION

During traffic stops, officers are permitted to request a driver's license, vehicle registration, and proof of insurance. These items relate directly to the purpose of the stop and fall within the officer's authority.

Outside a traffic setting, whether an officer may require identification depends on the state's laws. Some jurisdictions have "stop-and-identify" statutes, allowing an officer with reasonable suspicion to request a name. Even in these states the requirement is limited: the officer may ask for a name and basic identifying information, but generally may not demand answers to unrelated questions.

Citizens maintain the right to remain silent. Providing one's name when required is not the same as waiving constitutional rights beyond that limited obligation.

PAT-DOWNS FOR WEAPONS

When officers have reasonable suspicion that a person is armed and dangerous, they may perform a limited frisk. This is not a full search. It is a brief pat-down of outer clothing to check for weapons that could threaten safety.

The officer's purpose in a frisk is protection, not evidence gathering. Items unrelated to weapons may not be manipulated or examined unless their criminal nature is immediately apparent through touch. This boundary preserves the balance between officer safety and the citizen's Fourth Amendment protections.

SEARCHES REQUIRING CONSENT OR PROBABLE CAUSE

Most searches require either voluntary consent or probable cause. Officers may ask for permission to search a vehicle, bag, or personal belongings. Citizens have the right to refuse. Refusing consent cannot legally be used as evidence of wrongdoing.

If an officer has probable cause, a warrant is generally required—unless a recognized exception applies. *Vehicles fall under the "automobile exception," allowing warrantless searches when probable cause exists due to the vehicle's mobility.* Personal belongings usually require a warrant unless the search is part of a lawful arrest.

Understanding this distinction helps citizens recognize when their consent truly is voluntary and when a search is occurring under established legal authority.

DETENTION LIMITS

A detention during a stop must remain brief and tied to the reason for the stop. Officers may run computer checks, verify documents, and address safety concerns. They may not prolong the encounter without additional reasonable suspicion. Detention ends when the officer concludes the purpose of the stop. If the officer states that the person is free to leave, the encounter becomes voluntary. If the officer does not release the person and continues questioning without new justification, the detention may exceed lawful limits.

OFFICER SAFETY MEASURES
Legally speaking, officers may take reasonable steps to ensure safety during an encounter. This may include directing where a person stands, asking occupants to remain in or exit a vehicle, or temporarily separating individuals during a stop. These measures are permitted when they relate to safety and do not become punitive.

Instructions must remain reasonable. Commands aimed solely at ensuring order, minimizing risk, or clarifying communication fall within lawful authority. Interfering with these safety-related instructions may constitute obstruction under state law.

WHAT OFFICERS CANNOT DO
Officers may not search a person or vehicle without a lawful basis. They may not detain someone longer than necessary for the original purpose of the stop. They may not require a citizen to answer questions unrelated to the encounter's scope, other than identification where legally mandated. They cannot expand a stop into a broader investigation without specific, articulable facts. They may not use a person's refusal to consent to a search as evidence of wrongdoing. They cannot block recording from a non-interfering distance, nor may they retaliate against a citizen for remaining silent. They also may not use force except when objectively necessary. Any use of force must be proportional to the threat perceived at the moment.

SUMMARY
Police may stop individuals based on reasonable suspicion, request identification where authorized, and conduct limited pat-downs when safety requires it. Searches generally require consent or probable cause. Detentions must remain brief and tied to their purpose. Officers may take reasonable safety measures but must stay within constitutional limits. Note: Once a police stop begins, a citizen no longer has complete freedom of movement; that freedom is temporarily limited until the stop is resolved.

During brief detentions the law allows police to conduct limited protective safety checks, such as pat-downs, which help stabilize the encounter and ensure the safety of both parties. Illustration copyright © Lochlainn Seabrook.

CHAPTER 4

What You Are Allowed to do During Encounters

You have clear constitutional rights during any police encounter. This chapter explains how to use them in a calm, precise, and lawful manner. The goal is not to challenge an officer, but to help you understand the boundaries of your conduct and the protections already built into the law. It also clarifies what officers may reasonably expect from you, which reduces confusion in high-stress moments. Knowing these limits supports safer interactions for both sides. With this foundation, you can respond confidently while remaining fully within the law.

YOUR RIGHT TO REMAIN SILENT

Except in states where identification is required, you are not obligated to answer any questions. This right stems from the Fifth Amendment. You may decline to discuss where you are going, what you are doing, or whether you consent to a search. A simple statement is enough: "I am invoking my right to remain silent." Once stated, stop talking. (See Appendix F for important note.)

Silence cannot legally be treated as guilt. Officers may continue asking questions, but you do not have to respond. Remaining silent is a lawful choice and protects you from unintentionally providing unclear or inaccurate statements.

YOUR RIGHT TO ASK IF YOU ARE FREE TO LEAVE

In many encounters, police authority depends on whether you are being detained. You may ask, "Am I free to leave?" This question is lawful, appropriate, and clarifies the status of the encounter.

If the officer says you are free to go, walk away calmly. If the officer says you are being detained, do not panic. Remain still and follow instructions. Asking this question helps determine whether the officer's authority has shifted from a voluntary conversation to a lawful detention based on reasonable suspicion.

YOUR RIGHT TO REFUSE CONSENT TO SEARCHES

You can refuse a search of your person, vehicle, bags, or home, *unless an officer has probable cause, a warrant, or specific legal authority under an exception*. Refusing consent does not imply wrongdoing. A clear statement is sufficient: "I do not consent to any searches." Say it once, calmly. Do not physically block or resist. If the officer proceeds, your refusal preserves the issue for later legal review. This right protects privacy and ensures that searches follow constitutional standards. It also reduces the risk of misunderstandings during the encounter.

YOUR RIGHT TO RECORD THE ENCOUNTER

You may record police activity in public—as long as you do not interfere with the officer's duties. Recording from a safe distance is lawful. There is no nationwide rule requiring a specific number of feet (each state differs); the law focuses on whether your position allows officers to perform their work without obstruction.

Courts have upheld the right to record police—as long as you maintain a reasonable buffer and do not impede movement, communication, or safety decisions. A stable, non-intrusive position avoids any suggestion of interference. If officers feel you are too close or are interrupting their investigation, they may ask you to step back. Do so without comment or sudden movements, as failing to obey when instructed can be treated as interference, which, under state law, is defined as conduct that disrupts or complicates an officer's lawful duties. Do not reach abruptly into pockets or bags to retrieve your phone. Announce your intention before doing so. Officers are trained to monitor hand movements for safety reasons. A simple statement—such as, "I am going to record"—keeps the interaction predictable.

YOUR RIGHT TO DECLINE CONSENT TO FIELD SOBRIETY EXERCISES

During a traffic stop, officers may request field sobriety exercises. In many states you may decline these exercises without violating implied consent laws. Breath or chemical tests after a lawful arrest may involve different rules. If unsure, ask whether the request is mandatory. Officers must clarify whether a test is required under your state's laws. Calmly choosing not to perform voluntary exercises is within your rights.

YOUR RIGHT TO BE FREE FROM UNNECESSARY FORCE

Citizens are entitled to be treated with objectively reasonable force standards. *You cannot control an officer's decisions, but you can control your own conduct.* Keep hands visible, move slowly, and avoid any behavior that could be misinterpreted. If force is used unlawfully, the appropriate remedy is later review, not resistance during the encounter.

YOUR RIGHT TO ASK FOR A LAWYER

If questioning becomes custodial, you may request an attorney. Once requested, officers must stop questioning until counsel is present. The Sixth Amendment protects this right after formal charges, but asking for a lawyer earlier helps avoid errors or confusion. A brief, clear statement—"I want a lawyer"—is enough. Do not continue answering questions afterward.

YOUR RIGHT TO REMAIN POLITE & CONTROLLED

Calm behavior is not a legal right, but it is an effective exercise of your rights. Staying steady protects you from escalating a situation and keeps the encounter focused on lawful procedure. Officers respond better to predictable conduct. You retain the ability to express your position respectfully. You do not forfeit your rights by choosing courtesy. Remember that during a police stop the First Amendment only protects your free speech up to a certain point. For example, if it interferes or becomes threatening, it is not protected. (For a detailed discussion on this topic see Appendix E.)

WHAT YOU SHOULD AVOID DOING

Even when asserting rights, avoid sudden movements, raised tones, or argumentative posture. Do not reach into compartments or bags without warning. Do not provide false information or false identification. These actions can turn a lawful encounter into a criminal matter. Your objective is clarity. Assert rights cleanly, then stop elaborating.

SUMMARY

During any police encounter, you may remain silent, speak freely (with some exceptions), refuse consent to searches, ask if you are free to leave, record the interaction, request a lawyer, and politely decline voluntary exercises. These rights protect you, but they must be used calmly and without confrontation. Understanding your boundaries—and the officer's—keeps the encounter safe, predictable, and constitutionally grounded.

By law, during a pullover a citizen must provide the requested documents. However, he or she retains the right to remain silent, refuse consent for searches, record the encounter, and ask for an attorney. Outside these rights, the safest course of action is compliance, because lawful authority is often broader than people realize: investigative stops that escalate into detention or arrest trigger expanded police powers while reducing the citizen's ability to exercise certain rights. Illustration copyright © Lochlainn Seabrook.

CHAPTER 5

Traffic Stops: Step-by-Step

Most citizens encounter police for the first time on the road, which makes the traffic stop the most common point of contact with law enforcement. Important points:

- Because these moments unfold quickly, understanding each phase helps reduce uncertainty and keeps the encounter safe for everyone involved.
- Knowing what officers may request, what you must provide, and what remains optional clarifies your role.
- A clear grasp of the stop's limits protects your rights without creating tension. This framework also helps you respond calmly when conditions change.

Let us look at a typical nine-step sequence of events that begin once you are pulled over.

1. THE INITIAL SIGNAL
A traffic stop begins the moment an officer activates emergency lights or a siren. This is a lawful order to pull over. Choose a safe spot on the right side of the road, turn-signal your intention, and slow down steadily. Officers evaluate driver behavior from the instant the stop is initiated; calm, predictable movement supports safety on both sides while helping avoid misunderstandings later.

Important: Once you have stopped, put your vehicle in park, turn the engine off, place the keys on the dashboard, roll down the driver's side window, and put your hands on the steering wheel. Then simply await the arrival and instructions of the officer. And *always* remain in your vehicle—unless instructed otherwise.

2. OFFICER APPROACH & FIRST CONTACT
The officer's first priority is safety. Expect him or her to stand slightly behind your window, where they can observe the interior of the vehicle. They may greet you, identify themselves, and state the reason for the stop. You are permitted to remain silent, but

providing your name and basic identifying information during a lawful traffic stop is usually required under state law. The Fourth Amendment protects against unreasonable searches, but it does not bar an officer from asking questions or making observations from outside the vehicle.

3. REQUIRED DOCUMENTS
During a legitimate traffic stop, you must provide three items upon request: *driver's license, vehicle registration*, and *proof of insurance*. Moving slowly while narrating your actions—stating something like "My registration is in the glove box"—reduces anxiety and prevents misunderstandings.

Officers are allowed to verify the authenticity of your documents and check for outstanding warrants. This brief detention is lawful under established traffic-stop principles, so long as it is reasonably related to the purpose of the stop.

4. SCOPE & DURATION OF THE STOP
A traffic stop must remain tied to its original purpose. Officers may issue a warning or citation, run your information, and ensure the vehicle is properly registered and insured. They may not extend the stop without reasonable suspicion of an additional offense.

Reasonable suspicion is a specific, articulable basis for believing criminal activity may be occurring. It is a lower threshold than probable cause, but it must be grounded in observable facts. If no such factors exist, the officer must complete the traffic-related tasks and allow you to leave.

5. QUESTIONS & CONVERSATION
Officers are permitted to ask questions unrelated to the traffic violation, but you are not required to answer. The Fifth Amendment protects your right to remain silent. If you choose to use this right, a simple, calm statement such as "I prefer not to answer questions" is sufficient. Remaining polite avoids unnecessary tension. Silence alone does not create reasonable suspicion and should not prolong the stop (though see Appendix F).

6. SEARCHES & CONSENT
The officer may request permission to search your vehicle. Consent is voluntary and you are not required to grant it. You may decline with a neutral statement such as "I do not consent to searches." Without consent or probable cause—meaning a fair probability that evidence of a crime is present—officers cannot lawfully search the

interior of your car.

However, officers may look through your windows for anything clearly observable. In accordance with the "plain view" doctrine, items visible from the outside, or odors such as marijuana (in states where it remains contraband), may create probable cause.

7. REMOVAL FROM THE VEHICLE

For safety reasons officers may legally order drivers and passengers to step out of the vehicle. *This authority has been upheld by the courts and does not require individualized suspicion.* Complying with the order does not reduce your rights. Once outside the vehicle you may remain silent and you may refuse consent to searches. If asked to sit in the patrol car, you may politely decline—*unless* the officer directs you to do so for safety purposes or for lawful reasons tied to the stop.

8. PASSENGERS' RIGHTS

Passengers share the same constitutional protections as the driver. They must obey lawful orders related to safety, but they are not required to provide identification—*unless the officer has reasonable suspicion of a separate violation.* Passengers may ask if they are free to leave; if the officer confirms they are not being detained, they may depart on foot, unless instructed otherwise for safety.

9. ENDING THE STOP

The stop concludes when the officer returns your documents and states you are free to go. Do not drive away until this is clearly conveyed. The officer may offer advice or warnings, but once the traffic-related tasks are complete and no reasonable suspicion remains, legally your detention must come to an end.

SUMMARY

A traffic stop follows a predictable sequence: signal to pull over, wait for instructions, provide required documents, allow the officer to perform safety checks, and exercise your rights calmly. You may remain silent, decline consent to searches, and ask whether you are free to leave. Understanding these steps reduces uncertainty, keeps the focus on safety, and ensures that both citizens and officers follow established constitutional boundaries. Clear expectations also prevent small misunderstandings from growing into unnecessary tension. When you know what typically occurs during a stop you maintain awareness throughout the encounter. With this structure in mind the encounter stays controlled.

When an officer pulls you over the correct response is to turn off your engine, put the keys on the dashboard, roll down your window, and put your hands on the steering wheel. These actions help ensure the safety of everyone involved. Illustration copyright © Lochlainn Seabrook.

CHAPTER 6

Vehicle Searches

Police searches of vehicles follow a distinct set of constitutional rules that differ from searches of homes or personal belongings. Understanding these rules helps you stay calm, communicate clearly, and make informed decisions during a stop. It also clarifies when officers may search without a warrant and when they must rely on consent or probable cause. With this knowledge you can recognize the limits on each type of search and respond confidently.

THE LEGAL FOUNDATION

Vehicle searches fall primarily under the Fourth Amendment, which protects against unreasonable searches and seizures. *Because cars are mobile, however, courts recognize exceptions to the warrant requirement. These exceptions allow officers to search a vehicle under specific circumstances*—though each circumstance has boundaries. The central ideas are probable cause, consent, officer safety, and inventory procedures.

CONSENT SEARCHES

Many vehicle searches begin with a simple question: "Do you mind if I take a look inside?" If you say yes, you have given consent. Once consent is given, an officer may search areas reasonably connected to that consent. If you say no, the officer may not search unless another lawful basis exists.

Key points of consent:
• You are not required to agree.
• You do not need to justify your refusal.
• The refusal must be clear and calm.

An officer may continue to ask questions, but the lack of consent remains.

A polite, direct phrase—such as "I do not consent to any searches"—is enough. This preserves your rights without escalating the situation. Refusing consent does not give the officer probable cause. It simply means the officer must rely on another legal justification if a search is to occur.

PROBABLE CAUSE SEARCHES

Probable cause is a higher standard than reasonable suspicion. It means the officer has specific, factual reasons to believe evidence of a crime is inside the vehicle. These reasons must be objective and articulable. Examples that may create probable cause:

• The smell of contraband recognized by law enforcement.
• Visible evidence in plain view, such as open containers or objects whose specific characteristics reasonably indicate unlawful activity.
• Information from reliable sources that directly ties the vehicle to a crime.

If probable cause exists, an officer may search areas of your vehicle where the suspected evidence could reasonably be located. This can include the trunk, containers, and compartments. Probable cause does not allow an unlimited or destructive search, and officers must follow department policy regarding the handling of property.

SEARCHES FOR OFFICER SAFETY

Officers may conduct a limited search when specific facts support a reasonable belief that a person may be dangerous and could access a weapon. This principle stems from the same logic that governs protective pat-downs.

In a vehicle context this allows an officer to visually inspect areas within the driver's reach, such as the floorboard, center console, or glove compartment. The purpose is strictly safety-based. It is not a full search for evidence.

If the officer sees contraband or illegal items during this protective check, those items may be seized under the "plain view" doctrine if the discovery is lawful and unintentional.

INVENTORY SEARCHES

If your vehicle is lawfully impounded, police may conduct an inventory search. The purpose is administrative: to document the contents, protect your property, and safeguard officers from claims of theft or damage. The search must follow a standardized policy, not individual discretion.

Inventory searches do not require a warrant or probable cause, but they must stay within the bounds of established procedure and cannot be used as a pretext for a criminal investigation.

SEARCHES AFTER ARREST

When a person is arrested during a traffic stop, officers may search areas closely connected to the arrest if they reasonably believe there is evidence related to the offense. This is narrower than past interpretations and limited by modern judicial standards. For example, if the arrest is for a driving violation, officers generally may not search unrelated compartments unless there is an independent basis such as probable cause or officer safety concerns.

YOUR ROLE DURING A SEARCH

During any search—consensual or otherwise—your conduct should be composed and aimed at safety and clarity:

• Keep your hands visible.
• Avoid reaching for personal items unless instructed.
• Stay in the position the officer directs.
• Speak calmly and briefly.
• Do not interfere with the search, even if you believe it is unlawful.

If you think your rights were violated, the correct time to address it is *afterward* through legal channels. Challenging a search during the encounter can escalate the situation and place you at risk of additional legal or safety complications.

WHAT POLICE MAY NOT DO

Officers may not search your vehicle based solely on:

• Your refusal to consent.
• A "hunch" without factual support.
• General curiosity.
• Punitive motives.

They may not extend a stop for the sole purpose of seeking a search unless they develop reasonable suspicion of a separate offense. Detention must remain tied to the legitimate purpose of the original stop unless new information lawfully expands the scope.

They also may not pressure or coerce you into giving consent when you have the right to decline. They cannot use unrelated questioning to prolong the encounter beyond what the situation requires. Nor may they treat ordinary nervousness as automatic justification for a search or extended detention.

As an American citizen you can refuse to let the police search your vehicle. However, if an officer finds he has probable cause, such as the odor of contraband, visible illegal items, or incriminating statements, your right is overridden and a vehicle search may proceed. Illustration copyright © Lochlainn Seabrook.

CHAPTER 7

When Law Enforcement Comes to Your Door

A knock on your door from law enforcement creates a different kind of encounter than stops in public spaces. Here the threshold matters, because the home receives the strongest Fourth Amendment protection. Understanding what officers may do, what you may decline, and how to communicate clearly will keep the situation steady and predictable.

WHY OFFICERS COME TO A RESIDENCE
Officers may come to a home for several reasons:

• To ask questions about an investigation.
• To conduct a "knock-and-talk" interview.
• To serve a warrant.
• To check on a reported emergency or welfare concern.
• To locate a person believed to be inside.

Each purpose determines the level of authority the officer has when standing at your door.

THE THRESHOLD & ITS PROTECTIONS
The Fourth Amendment places the home at the top of its privacy hierarchy. Without a warrant, consent, or an emergency, officers may not enter. Opening your door does not remove this protection. You retain full control over whether entry occurs unless a lawful exception applies.

If officers have no warrant, their authority is limited to speaking with you. They may request information, ask for consent to enter, or ask if someone else is inside. You may answer or decline. You may also choose to step outside and close the door behind you, which maintains the barrier.

THE "KNOCK-AND-TALK"

A "knock-and-talk" is a voluntary interview. Officers knock, identify themselves, and attempt to obtain information or consent. You are not required to open your door. If you choose to speak, you may keep the conversation brief and remain polite. Officers may stand where any member of the public may stand—your porch, walkway, or driveway. They may not wander around the property without a warrant, consent, or an emergency exception.

An officer may not block your door or place a foot in your doorway; this is considered "unlawful entry" and is a violation of the Fourth Amendment. If this occurs, do not resist—state clearly that you do not consent and wait for the officer to step back. If the officer refuses, remain calm and repeat that you do not consent.

WARRANTS: WHAT THEY ALLOW

If officers bring a search warrant, they may enter even if you object. A search warrant must specify the location and the items or persons to be seized. You may ask to see it, and they must provide it. Do not interfere with the execution of a warrant. You may observe from a safe position and may remain silent. You retain the right to consult an attorney.

If officers bring an arrest warrant, they may enter the home of the person named in the warrant if they reasonably believe that person is inside. If the arrest warrant is for someone else, officers typically need consent or a search warrant to enter your home unless an emergency exists.

EXIGENT CIRCUMSTANCES

Certain emergencies allow officers to enter without a warrant. These include:

• Immediate threats to life or safety.
• Hot pursuit of a fleeing suspect.
• Evidence at imminent risk of destruction.
• Fires or medical emergencies.

These exceptions are narrow and must be justified by real, immediate circumstances. Once the emergency ends, so does the exception.

CONSENT: WHAT IT MEANS
Consent removes the need for a warrant. If you agree to let officers enter, the scope of their entry and search is defined by the permission you give. You may limit consent to specific rooms or deny consent entirely. Consent must be voluntary, not coerced. You may withdraw consent at any time—*unless probable cause has arisen*. Once officers are inside anything in plain view may be inspected or documented under standard Fourth Amendment rules.

SPEAKING WITH OFFICERS
You may speak or remain silent. The Fifth Amendment protects you from being compelled to answer questions that could be used against you. A polite, simple statement such as, "I choose not to answer questions," is sufficient. Provide identification only when required by law, which is rare inside the home unless tied to a warrant or specific state statutes. Remain composed and respectful.

IF THEY ASK TO SEARCH
Without a warrant or a valid exception, a search requires your consent. Officers may ask directly or indirectly. You may decline without argument by saying, "I do not consent to any searches." This preserves your rights and keeps the exchange orderly. Declining consent is not obstruction.

DOCUMENTING THE ENCOUNTER
You may record officers from your doorway as long as you do not obstruct them. Remain stationary, keep your hands visible, and do not interfere with their movements. Recording should be done calmly and without commentary.

IF YOU STEP OUTSIDE
For legal and safety reasons it is not recommended that you step outside to talk to officers. However, if you choose to, close the door behind you. This maintains the boundary and prevents implied consent. Officers may not restrict your movement during a knock-and-talk; if they do, the encounter has become a detention.

SUMMARY
When police come to your door, the home's constitutional protection guides the encounter. Officers may request information or consent, but you choose whether to allow entry. Calm communication helps keep the situation controlled, and using your rights respectfully maintains stability.

During a "knock-and-talk," officers may request information or consent outside your door. But only a valid warrant or an emergency permits entry without permission. Illustration copyright © Lochlainn Seabrook.

CHAPTER 8

Your Rights When Recording Police

Encounters with law enforcement often occur suddenly, and the ability to document them has become an important aspect of modern public life. *Recording police activity is lawful when carried out responsibly.* This chapter explains how that right works, what limits apply, and how to exercise it without interfering with legitimate police duties.

THE CONSTITUTIONAL BASIS FOR RECORDING
The right to record police activity arises from long-established protections surrounding the First Amendment, freedom of expression and the gathering of information. Courts have consistently recognized that documenting how public officials perform their duties serves an important public function. When an encounter takes place in a location where you are already permitted to be, you may observe and record without asking for permission.

This right applies whether you are involved in the encounter or are simply a bystander. The key requirement is that your recording does not obstruct the officer's work or jeopardize safety.

THE SCOPE OF THE RIGHT
You may begin recording at any point during an encounter. Officers may ask questions about your actions, but they cannot order you to stop solely because they prefer not to be filmed. Recording an event is not, by itself, interference. You do not need to state a reason for recording, and you do not need to justify your presence if you are in a public area where you may lawfully stand.

Officers remain free to conduct their duties, and your presence must not hinder those duties. *As long as your actions are calm, predictable, and do not intrude into the operational space of the officers, your recording is lawful.*

NO REQUIREMENT FOR PERMISSION
You are not required to ask an officer whether you may record. Police cannot impose conditions on recording that stem only from

personal discomfort. Any instruction that restricts your recording must relate to safety, scene control, or prevention of interference. A request to stop filming based on preference or convenience exceeds an officer's lawful authority.

If the officer believes your position is too close or hazardous, they may instruct you to move. Complying with the instruction does not require you to stop recording.

DISTANCE & SAFE POSITIONING

There is no nationwide legal rule dictating a specific number of feet you must stand from an officer while recording. Instead, courts rely on the principle of non-interference. Officers may direct you to maintain a safe distance so that your presence does not obstruct their movements or distract them during sensitive tasks.

The required distance varies by circumstance. High-risk stops, unstable scenes, crowds, and confined areas may require additional space. The standard is whether your proximity could reasonably impede the officer's work. Recording from a stable position, without advancing toward officers or entering restricted zones, reduces the possibility of conflict.

MAINTAINING VISIBILITY & PREDICTABILITY

If you decide to record, make your actions clear. Officers monitor hand movements, especially during uncertain or tense encounters. Before reaching for your phone or camera, briefly announce your intention. Retrieve your device slowly and keep your hands visible. Avoid sudden steps toward officers or individuals being detained, and do not enter the path where officers are moving.

A steady posture, predictable gestures, and calm demeanor communicate that you are observing rather than participating in the encounter.

RESTRICTIONS ON POLICE ACTION

Officers may not seize, view, or delete your recordings without lawful justification. A belief that the footage might contain evidence does not automatically allow seizure. Established legal procedures—such as warrants or recognized exceptions—must guide any attempt to secure your device.

Police may not punish or threaten you simply for recording. Retaliation based solely on filming is not lawful. The line between a valid safety instruction and retaliation rests on whether the officer's command is tied to an objective operational need.

WHAT POLICE MAY REQUIRE

Officers may establish boundaries around an incident scene. These boundaries apply to everyone present and may include instructions to stand back, remain behind a barrier, or avoid a specific area. If the scene is unstable officers may restrict entry entirely. These restrictions remain valid even when you are recording, provided they are connected to safety, evidence preservation, or scene control.

If you are the individual being detained or questioned, you may record while also complying with all lawful commands. The officer may instruct you to keep your hands visible or remain in a particular position; but these commands cannot be used to prevent recording unless safety is genuinely at stake.

A NOTE ABOUT SOUND & PRIVATE LOCATIONS

Recording police inside your home carries different considerations. If the encounter occurs at your door or inside your residence, you may record as long as the recording does not interfere with the officer's lawful purpose. Outside the home, most states allow open recording of both video and audio in public settings because there is no reasonable expectation of privacy during police duties performed openly.

BEST PRACTICES FOR EFFECTIVE RECORDING

When recording, remain stationary, avoid verbal confrontation, and refrain from giving instructions to others at the scene. Focus on documenting the encounter rather than influencing it. If an officer directs you to move back or adjust your position, comply while continuing to film. If your recording captures sensitive information—such as injured individuals or private details—handle and store the footage responsibly.

Clear, minimal communication reduces misunderstanding. If you need to assert your right to record, do so briefly and respectfully.

SUMMARY

Recording police in public is lawful when it does not interfere with their duties. You do not need permission to film, and officers cannot stop you, unless safety concerns require repositioning. There is no fixed national distance rule, but you must maintain a reasonable buffer. Officers may not seize or delete your footage without lawful cause. Calm conduct helps you document the encounter while preserving your rights.

Filming the police is legal—but there are limitations. Know the laws in your area before attempting to record law enforcement. In all cases, remain at a safe and respectful distance and do not interfere. If you are asked to "step back," do so calmly and quietly. Illustration copyright © Lochlainn Seabrook.

CHAPTER 9

Miranda Rights Explained Simply

U nderstanding when your rights apply during questioning can make the difference between a calm interaction and an avoidable problem. Miranda rules set the boundary between voluntary conversation and legally protected silence. This chapter explains how that boundary works, when it activates, and what both you and officers may do once questioning begins.

WHAT MIRANDA IS

Miranda rights arise from long-standing constitutional protections. The Fifth Amendment bars compelled self-incrimination. The Sixth Amendment protects the right to counsel. Miranda warnings do not create new rights; they simply remind a person that these rights already exist. The warning must be given only when two conditions are present at the same time: *custody* and *interrogation*. Without both, officers are not required to issue the warning.

CUSTODY: WHEN IT BEGINS

Custody occurs when a reasonable person would believe they are not free to leave. It does not require handcuffs or a formal arrest. Being placed in the back of a patrol car, being surrounded in a confined space, or being told you must stay in one location can all qualify. A routine traffic stop usually does not. Detention for investigative purposes may feel restrictive, but courts treat such stops as temporary and not custodial; unless the situation becomes significantly more controlled or prolonged. If officers move you to a different location, restrict your movement beyond what is necessary for safety, or communicate that you are not permitted to end the encounter, custody may have begun.

INTERROGATION: WHAT IT MEANS

Interrogation includes direct questioning and any statement designed to elicit an incriminating response. Casual conversation is not interrogation unless the questions relate to suspected wrongdoing. Officers may ask for identification, licenses, registration, or routine safety information without issuing a warning. These requests are administrative, not investigative. Once questioning shifts toward your involvement in a potential offense, Miranda rules may come into play if custody also exists.

WHEN THE WARNING MUST BE GIVEN
Officers must give the familiar warning—right to remain silent, anything said can be used in court, right to an attorney, and the ability to have one appointed—before conducting custodial interrogation. *If either element is missing—custody or interrogation—the warning is not required.* You may still choose not to speak, and you may still request an attorney even if the officer has not read the warning. The absence of a warning does not invalidate an arrest. It only affects whether your statements may be used in court.

YOUR RIGHT TO REMAIN SILENT
You may decline to answer questions at any time. Silence must be communicated clearly. A simple statement such as "I am exercising my right to remain silent" is enough. After you invoke this right officers must stop questioning. They may still address matters unrelated to the investigation, such as safety instructions or procedural steps. Remaining silent without clearly stating you are choosing to remain silent may be perceived as uncertainty and lead to legal issues (see Appendix F), so express your choice plainly.

YOUR RIGHT TO AN ATTORNEY
You may request an attorney as soon as you feel questioning is moving into areas where legal guidance is necessary. A clear statement such as "I want to speak with an attorney before answering questions" is required. Once this right is invoked, officers must stop all questioning until counsel is present. You may not be pressured into continuing. If you voluntarily restart the conversation without prompting, questioning may resume, but only after confirming that you understand your rights.

WAIVING YOUR RIGHTS
You may choose to answer questions after receiving the warning. A waiver must be voluntary, knowing, and intelligent. Officers may confirm that you understand the warning. You are not required to sign any form. You may also stop answering at any time. A waiver given under threats, promises, or coercion is not valid. The law focuses on whether your choice is clear and voluntary, ensuring that

any statement you give is genuinely your own.

QUESTIONS OFFICERS MAY STILL ASK
Even during custody, officers may ask certain administrative questions without providing a warning. These include requests for identification, inquiries related to officer or public safety, and basic biographical information needed for booking. These questions are narrow and must not be used as a way to obtain incriminating information. If an officer's question is designed to produce a confession or admission, the Miranda warning must come first.

PRACTICAL GUIDANCE FOR CITIZENS
If you are uncertain whether you are free to leave, you may ask directly. If questioning becomes investigative and you prefer not to speak, calmly invoke your rights. Avoid raising your voice, arguing, or refusing lawful instructions. Invoking your rights is not an act of resistance. It is a lawful, protected action. Keep your hands visible, follow safety commands, and speak clearly and respectfully.

PRACTICAL GUIDANCE FOR OFFICERS
Officers must balance investigative needs with constitutional limits. *Confirming identity, maintaining safety, and asking routine questions are all permissible.* Once custody and interrogation combine, a warning must be issued. Officers are expected to recognize clear invocations of silence or counsel. Continuing to question after a clear invocation can invalidate statements and undermine an otherwise lawful investigation.

WHAT MIRANDA DOES NOT COVER
Miranda does not affect physical evidence, the legality of a stop, or the lawfulness of an arrest. It does not prevent officers from securing a scene or giving safety commands. It does not guarantee release if you choose not to speak. It governs questioning under custodial circumstances—not the broader range of police duties.

SUMMARY
Miranda rights protect you from compelled statements during custodial questioning. *The warning is required only when custody and interrogation occur together.* You may remain silent and request an attorney at any stage. Clear communication, calm behavior, and understanding the limits of both citizen rights and police authority help keep these encounters controlled and predictable. Invoking your rights plainly ensures they are recognized and enforced.

Mirandizing informs a person in custody of their constitutional rights prior to official questioning, ensuring any statements are voluntary and legally admissible. In this way Miranda rights protect both the individual and the officers involved. Illustration copyright © Lochlainn Seabrook.

CHAPTER 10

Arrests: What Happens Next?

An arrest marks a formal change in a police encounter. Once an officer decides to take someone into custody, the encounter stops being a brief investigation and becomes a defined legal process. Knowing how this process works reduces uncertainty and clarifies what will follow.

WHEN AN ARREST IS LAWFULLY MADE

An arrest occurs when an officer restrains your movement with the intent to take you into custody. This requires probable cause, meaning clear facts that would lead a reasonable person to believe you have committed, are committing, or are about to commit a crime. Probable cause is stronger than the reasonable suspicion used for temporary stops.

Officers may arrest without a warrant if the offense occurred in their presence or if state law allows it. When acting on a warrant, they must identify themselves and state that a warrant exists, though they are not required to display it immediately. *Officers are not required to state the reason for the arrest at that moment; they need only provide the explanation within a reasonable time.*

WHAT TO EXPECT DURING THE ARREST

You will be told that you are under arrest and given instructions. Officers may handcuff you as a standard safety measure. This does not imply guilt; it is routine in custodial situations.

Your safest approach is to follow instructions, avoid sudden movements, and keep a steady tone. Officers must control the environment, and cooperation reduces the chance of misunderstanding. *Officers need not and generally do not discuss legal matters or debate the charges during an arrest; legal questions belong to the courts and thus come later in the process.*

If you are arrested officers may conduct a limited search. Officers may check for weapons, contraband, and evidence within reach. The search is limited to your person and the immediate area. Bags or personal items may be secured and inventoried.

YOUR RIGHTS AFTER BEING DETAINED

After arrest, your constitutional protections remain in place. You have the right to remain silent and may refuse to answer questions about the incident. Basic identifying information may be required by state law, but anything beyond that is optional. You also have the right to consult an attorney. If custodial interrogation begins, officers must advise you of the Miranda protections. You may state that you want to remain silent or that you want a lawyer. Once invoked, questioning must stop unless you choose to resume it.

TRANSPORTATION & BOOKING

After the scene is secured, you will likely be transported to a detention facility. Transport procedures follow safety rules designed to protect everyone involved.

At the facility the booking process begins. This includes recording identifying information, taking fingerprints, photographing you, and securing property. These steps create an official record and ensure accountability.

Phone calls, including to an attorney, generally occur only *after* booking and according to facility rules. The right to counsel does not provide immediate phone access during the arrest itself.

SEARCHES OF PERSONAL BELONGINGS

All property in your possession will be inventoried. This administrative search documents what you had at the time of arrest and prevents disputes.

If a vehicle is involved it may be towed or secured. An inventory search of the vehicle may occur if required by policy. *This does not require consent*, but must follow written procedures. Evidence found during a lawful inventory may still be used.

INITIAL APPEARANCE & CHARGES

The law requires that an arrested person be taken before a judge within a reasonable time. During this initial appearance charges are presented and rights for the next stage are explained. The judge may consider conditions for release, including bond or recognizance. This stage does not determine guilt; it ensures due process and establishes the path forward.

YOUR RIGHT TO COUNSEL

After booking and processing you may have an attorney at all subsequent critical stages. If you cannot afford one the court can appoint counsel. Requests to contact an attorney or a family member are handled under facility rules, and access may be supervised or briefly delayed, but must remain reasonable. Once represented, communication regarding the case should go through your lawyer.

WHAT OFFICERS MAY & MAY NOT DO
Officers may use reasonable force, apply restraints, conduct safety searches, transport you, and complete administrative tasks. They may ask questions, but you may decline to answer beyond identifying information unless state law requires more.

They may not use excessive force, threaten punishment, or search areas without lawful authority. Their actions must remain within constitutional limits.

WHAT YOU SHOULD AVOID
Do not resist, argue, or attempt to negotiate your way out of custody. These actions increase risk and may lead to additional charges. Calm cooperation protects your safety while your rights protect your legal position. Providing false information or attempting to conceal or destroy evidence can cause serious complications. Even minor interference may be viewed as obstructive and can add new issues and charges. *Do not try to "clear things up" or seek legal explanations at the scene, as these matters fall outside the police's purview.* A reserved approach keeps the encounter predictable and protects your position.

IF YOU BELIEVE YOUR RIGHTS WERE VIOLATED
Concerns about the arrest should be handled *afterward through legal channels.* Document what you remember once safe to do so. Your attorney can challenge probable cause, search limits, or procedural errors before a judge.

Raising objections during the encounter almost never changes the outcome and will likely complicate matters. Waiting until you have legal advice ensures any challenge is made in the proper forum with the detail it requires.

SUMMARY
An arrest begins a structured legal process. Officers must have probable cause and follow established safety and administrative procedures. You retain the right to remain silent, the right to counsel, and the right to due process. Calm behavior and awareness of your rights guide you through the early stages of the process and preserve the clarity of the record for any legal review that follows.

A lawful arrest requires probable cause, such as public intoxication. Officers will state the charge when practical, secure the individual safely, and transport them for booking, at which time identification is confirmed, charges are recorded, and access to counsel follows. Illustration copyright © Lochlainn Seabrook.

CHAPTER 11

Understanding the Law Enforcement Perspective

Police encounters operate within a structured set of duties, safety concerns, and legal boundaries. Recognizing how officers approach these moments helps clarify why certain questions are asked, why specific movements matter, and why procedures may feel rigid. This chapter explains those elements without excusing unlawful conduct and without diminishing your constitutional rights. Its purpose is to give you an informed picture of what is happening on the other side of the interaction.

THE ROLE OF OFFICER SAFETY

Every police encounter begins with a fundamental obligation: ensuring that no one is harmed. Officers are trained to assess risk immediately, even during routine stops. They watch for visible weapons, sudden movements, or signs that someone may flee.

These assessments are not personal judgments about character; they are standard safety measures applied in every encounter. Understanding this helps you interpret why officers sometimes issue firm, repetitive instructions.

Clear hands, slow movements, and calm communication support this safety framework. They also reduce misunderstandings that could escalate tension. None of these expectations override your rights. But cooperating with basic safety directions keeps the situation predictable for both you and the officer.

WHY QUESTIONS ARE ASKED

Officers ask questions to determine what level of engagement is required. Initial questions are usually designed to identify who they are speaking with and whether any immediate concerns exist. The tone of the questions may seem brisk, but their purpose is to gather essential information quickly.

You are not required to answer every question, though *you must provide identification during lawful traffic stops and comply with basic commands related to safety*. If you choose to invoke your Fifth Amendment right to remain silent, do so politely. Stating that you are exercising this right is sufficient.

THE BASIS FOR DETENTION

Short detentions stem from the legal principle known as *reasonable suspicion*. This standard, recognized in Terry v. Ohio, allows officers to momentarily stop individuals to investigate potential criminal activity based on specific, articulable facts. It does not allow for lengthy questioning, unwarranted searches, or indefinite delays.

Reasonable suspicion is not the same as probable cause. The former supports brief inquiry, not full searches of your vehicle or belongings. Officers must have stronger justification to go further. If a detention expands beyond its purpose, you still retain the right to refuse consent to searches and to limit your answers to basic identifying information.

PROBABLE CAUSE & SEARCHES

Probable cause arises when officers have a reasonable belief, supported by facts, that a crime has occurred or that criminal evidence may be present. This standard governs the authority to conduct searches without a warrant in limited circumstances, including certain vehicle searches. Officer safety also permits a protective frisk when specific facts indicate a possible weapon.

You are never required to consent to a search. Declining consent does not create probable cause. If officers proceed without your permission, the legality of their decision is reviewed later by a court, not resolved at the roadside. Staying calm, avoiding argument, and clearly stating that you do not consent is the safest approach.

COMMUNICATION FROM THE OFFICER'S VIEW

Police communication is shaped by the need to maintain order while respecting constitutional boundaries. Officers often rely on short, direct statements because clarity reduces the risk of confusion. Interrupting instructions, talking over commands, or making unexpected movements complicates this process and may trigger additional safety checks.

If you do not understand an instruction, you may ask for clarification. Doing so calmly is important. Officers are trained to respond to clear requests for explanation without treating them as resistance. Mutual clarity helps both sides proceed safely.

WHY ENCOUNTERS SOMETIMES FEEL FORMAL

The formality of police encounters is intentional. Structured procedure prevents misunderstandings and helps officers document their actions accurately. This discipline also protects your rights by creating predictable steps: the reason for the stop, the request for documents, limited questioning, and the conclusion of the encounter.

Formality does not diminish your rights. You may remain silent, refuse consent to searches, and ask if you are free to leave. You may not, however, interfere with lawful instructions related to safety or identification requirements during traffic stops. This framework keeps the encounter consistent for both sides.

PAUSES, WAIT TIMES, & OFFICER DECISION-MAKING

Officers sometimes step away from your vehicle or pause before giving further instructions. These moments usually relate to verifying information, checking records, or coordinating with other units. They do not automatically indicate suspicion. Remaining patient and still during these brief intervals keeps the encounter stable. *If additional officers arrive, their presence often merely reflects procedural caution rather than an accusation of wrongdoing or the potential seriousness of the situation. Additional officers allow the primary officer or the contact officer to focus on communication while others maintain safety.*

Understanding the law enforcement perspective helps reduce uncertainty during police encounters. Officers are trained to prioritize safety and follow established procedures. You retain your rights throughout the encounter, including the right to remain silent and the right to refuse consent to searches. Remember that officers may still search without consent when the law provides independent authority, such as probable cause or a justified safety check.

Calm behavior, clear communication, and awareness of safety protocols make the interaction safer for everyone. Recognizing common patterns in officer behavior helps you anticipate what may happen next.

An accident response shows how police document events, divide tasks, and balance communication with scene safety and other officers. Being aware of these practices offers a clear view of the law enforcement perspective. Illustration copyright © Lochlainn Seabrook.

CHAPTER 12

Common Myths About Police Encounters

Misunderstandings about police encounters often arise from secondhand stories, outdated assumptions, and incorrect interpretations of constitutional rights. Clarifying these police-related myths helps prevent unnecessary conflict, protects your legal position, and keeps the interaction steady. This chapter examines the nine most frequent misconceptions and explains the factual rules that apply in real-world situations.

MYTH 1: YOU MUST ANSWER EVERY QUESTION

A common misunderstanding is that citizens must respond to all questions during a stop. While officers may ask for information, the Constitution protects your right to remain silent. During a lawful traffic stop you must provide your driver's license, registration, and proof of insurance when asked. Beyond these required items, answering additional questions is voluntary. You may decline politely and state that you are choosing to remain silent. Exercising this right should be done calmly, without raising your voice or appearing confrontational.

MYTH 2: REFUSING CONSENT TO A SEARCH LOOKS SUSPICIOUS

Some people believe that declining a search will automatically make an officer think they are hiding something. In reality, the law gives you the right to refuse consent, and exercising that right does not create probable cause. Officers understand that consent is voluntary. An officer may still conduct a search if another legal justification exists, but your refusal itself cannot serve as that justification. Stating "I do not consent to any searches" is sufficient, and you do not need to elaborate. (For more on this topic, see Appendix G.)

MYTH 3: YOU CAN DEMAND THAT AN OFFICER EXPLAIN ALL ACTIONS IMMEDIATELY

Although officers must provide the reason for a stop, *they are not required to pause an encounter to answer every question as it arises.* Their primary responsibilities are safety and lawful procedure. If an officer does not answer a question right away, it may be because they are managing multiple tasks or ensuring that the scene remains secure. Once the immediate duties are complete, officers typically explain the purpose and scope of the stop. You may ask for clarification at an appropriate time and in a steady tone.

MYTH 4: YOU ARE FREE TO LEAVE UNLESS FORMALLY TOLD YOU ARE BEING DETAINED

Many people assume that silence from an officer means they are free to walk or drive away. Legally you are considered detained during a traffic stop or investigative stop until the officer indicates otherwise. You may ask, "Am I free to leave?" If the officer says yes, the stop is concluded. If the answer is no, you must remain in place. Attempting to leave during a lawful detention can escalate the situation quickly and may lead to additional charges.

MYTH 5: IF YOU DID NOTHING WRONG, YOU CAN REFUSE ALL INSTRUCTIONS

Believing you are innocent, or actually being innocent, of wrongdoing does not remove the requirement to follow lawful commands connected to safety and identification. You are still obligated to follow an officer's instructions. For example, he or she may direct you to keep your hands visible, step out of the vehicle, or remain seated. These actions help stabilize the encounter. Refusing such instructions can be interpreted as interference, regardless of your intentions. Your rights—such as remaining silent or refusing consent to a search—remain intact, but they do not override safety-based commands.

MYTH 6: A TRAFFIC STOP IS AUTOMATICALLY AN ARREST

A traffic stop is a temporary detention, not an arrest. It is limited to addressing the reason for the stop and resolving safety concerns. Officers may check documents, verify information, and issue a citation or warning. An arrest requires probable cause that a crime has been committed. Most stops end without an arrest, and the encounter remains limited in scope when officers stay focused on the stated purpose of the stop. Knowing this distinction helps you gauge what to expect during the interaction.

MYTH 7: YOU CAN RECORD ONLY IF YOU ANNOUNCE IT

Citizens often think they must declare that they are recording an encounter. While being open about it can reduce confusion, there is no legal requirement to announce recording as long as you are in a place you have a right to be and you do not interfere with the officer's duties. Keeping your movements slow and your device visible helps prevent misunderstandings. If asked, you may confirm that you are recording.

MYTH 8: OFFICERS CANNOT ASK YOU TO STEP OUT OF YOUR VEHICLE

Officers may direct a driver or passenger to exit the vehicle during a lawful traffic stop. Courts recognize this authority for safety reasons. Exiting does not mean you are under arrest, and it does not remove your ability to remain silent or decline consent to searches. Complying keeps the encounter controlled and reduces miscommunication. Remaining steady as you step out helps the officer assess the scene. Once outside, you may continue to exercise your rights respectfully.

MYTH 9: DISAGREEING WITH AN OFFICER IS ILLEGAL

Polite disagreement is not unlawful. You may express your position clearly—as long as it does not interfere with the officer's ability to perform their duties. *Raising your voice, refusing safety-based instructions, or physically obstructing the officer's movements is different from verbal disagreement and may be considered interference.* Keeping communication calm preserves your rights and prevents unnecessary escalation. Staying measured also helps distinguish lawful expression from disruptive conduct. A steady tone allows the encounter to continue within clear constitutional boundaries.

MYTH 10: YOU CAN BE ARRESTED FOR INSULTING AN OFFICER

Many citizens think that disrespectful or emotional remarks during a stop can lead to arrest; but speech alone is protected unless it contains a true threat or obstructs the officer's work. Police training stresses *verbal professionalism*—sometimes called *verbal immunity* or *officer neutrality*—which teaches officers to ignore personal insults, maintain emotional distance, and stay focused on safety and procedure rather than pride and self-esteem. Because of this, frustration or rudeness from a citizen is not treated as grounds for escalation. These doctrines help prevent unnecessary conflict and support safer, more stable encounters.

A calm roadside stop shows how appearance and demeanor can create assumptions on both sides, highlighting the gap between popular myths and real police procedure. Illustration copyright © Lochlainn Seabrook.

CHAPTER 13

Historical Misconceptions About Policing in America

Public discussions about policing sometimes rely on simplified narratives that overlook how law enforcement actually developed in the United States. Misconceptions often arise from selective retellings or from assuming modern policing structures existed unchanged in earlier periods. This chapter clarifies eight common misunderstandings and explains how historical context influences present-day encounters.

MYTH 1: MODERN POLICING HAS ALWAYS OPERATED UNDER A CENTRAL NATIONAL SYSTEM

A common misconception is that American policing began as a unified national institution. In reality, policing developed locally, with sheriffs, constables, and watchmen operating independently and shaping their duties around community needs. The U.S. Constitution supported this structure by limiting federal authority and leaving most law-enforcement functions to states and municipalities. This history explains why police procedures and resources still differ from place to place today.

MYTH 2: EARLY POLICE FORCES HAD THE SAME LEGAL POWERS AS TODAY

Another misconception assumes that early American officers possessed the same legal framework, training standards, and procedural expectations that exist now. In earlier periods, authority was more limited and less standardized. Courts had not yet developed the detailed constitutional doctrines that guide modern policing, such as the rules surrounding searches, seizures, reasonable suspicion, and probable cause. Much of what shapes police encounters today—such as the protections of the Fourth Amendment as applied through later case law—evolved gradually through judicial interpretation. These expansions form the backbone of modern citizen protections.

MYTH 3: TRAFFIC ENFORCEMENT HAS ALWAYS BEEN A CORE POLICE FUNCTION

Traffic laws and the officers who enforce them are relatively recent developments. Early American communities had no motor vehicles, and therefore no vehicle-related regulations. As cars became common in the early 20th Century, states created licensing systems, roadway rules, and specialized enforcement duties. These changes transformed the nature of routine police encounters.

Today's traffic stop procedures, document requirements, and safety expectations originate from this shift, not from colonial or early republic traditions.

MYTH 4: CONSTITUTIONAL RIGHTS WERE ALWAYS APPLIED THE SAME WAY

Many assume the Constitution has always been enforced uniformly during police encounters. In reality, constitutional protections strengthened over time as courts clarified the Fourth Amendment, Fifth Amendment, and Sixth Amendment. Key decisions on detention, the right to remain silent, and limits on warrantless searches were developed well after the nation's founding.

This evolution explains why today's procedures feel highly structured—they reflect rules shaped through generations of case law.

MYTH 5: POLICE HAVE ALWAYS USED MODERN SAFETY PROTOCOLS

Contemporary officer-safety practices, such as maintaining visibility of hands, conducting protective frisks, or positioning vehicles in specific ways during traffic stops, did not exist in earlier eras. They arose from experience, training developments, and studies of officer-involved incidents.

These protocols are now routine because they reduce risk for both citizens and officers. Recognizing that these practices are newer than many assume helps explain why stops sometimes feel formal or procedural.

MYTH 6: HISTORICAL POLICING RELIED PRIMARILY ON FORCE

There is a misconception that early policing operated mainly through physical coercion. Historical records show that most early law-enforcement efforts focused on community order, basic crime prevention, and the enforcement of local regulations. Officers depended heavily on communication, personal familiarity with residents, and limited resources. Modern policing, despite its more structured framework, still retains these foundational concepts: clear communication, defined authority, and measured responses guided by law.

MYTH 7: ARREST PRACTICES HAVE ALWAYS BEEN THE SAME

In earlier periods arrest procedures were far simpler and far less regulated. Today, officers must meet specific constitutional standards before placing someone in custody, including establishing probable cause and respecting a detainee's rights. Documentation requirements, procedural safeguards, and judicial oversight developed over time to ensure transparency. These safeguards protect citizens and help maintain a consistent process throughout the country.

MYTH 8: CITIZENS OF THE PAST HAD FEWER RIGHTS DURING ENCOUNTERS

Although earlier Americans did not benefit from modern case law, they did possess fundamental legal protections. The rights to due process, to be free from unreasonable searches, and to remain silent existed in principle from the U.S. Constitution's adoption. What changed over time was how these rights were enforced and clarified. Modern policing reflects a more detailed system that defines the boundaries of detention, arrest, and search authority with greater precision.

SUMMARY

Misunderstandings about the history of policing can influence how citizens interpret modern encounters. American law enforcement did not begin as a unified national system, and many modern procedures emerged through gradual legal and practical developments. Constitutional protections expanded over time, shaping the structured framework that governs stops, detentions, and searches. Recognizing these historical realities supports clearer expectations and safer, more predictable interactions.

Error-filled modern depictions of early policing have helped shape public misconceptions about the origins of American law enforcement, emphasizing spectacle over reality and, unfortunately, influencing how it is still viewed by many today. Illustration copyright © Lochlainn Seabrook.

CHAPTER 14

The Path Forward: Good Citizenship & Good Policing

M oving forward with a clear understanding of rights and responsibilities depends on recognizing that *safe encounters require cooperation from both citizens and officers*. Each side has duties rooted in law rather than preference, and these duties shape how everyday interactions unfold. This chapter outlines how citizens can protect their rights while supporting stable, predictable encounters, and how lawful policing practices reinforce this balance.

THE FOUNDATION OF GOOD CITIZENSHIP

Good citizenship begins with awareness. Knowing your rights, your obligations, and the limits of police authority creates a solid base for calm decision-making. When citizens understand what officers are required to do during a stop, uncertainty fades. Producing requested documents, keeping movements slow, and communicating clearly help stabilize any encounter. These actions do not weaken your rights; they help preserve them.

Understanding what the law expects from you also prevents common mistakes. Refusing a lawful command, interrupting instructions, or moving unpredictably can change the tone of an encounter quickly. Good citizenship means exercising your rights firmly but politely, never confrontationally. It means using your knowledge to create a calm safe atmosphere rather than tension.

THE FOUNDATION OF GOOD POLICING

Good policing relies on lawful procedure and consistent adherence to constitutional boundaries. Officers are trained to manage risk, gather necessary information, and follow established rules. These procedures—however structured they may feel—protect both sides. When officers adhere to lawful standards, citizens can rely on predictable steps: the reason for the stop, clear instructions, limited questioning, and closure of the encounter once the purpose is complete.

Good policing also requires communication. A straightforward explanation of the reason for the stop, firm but courteous instructions, and clarity about next steps help citizens understand what is happening. These practices build trust, not through sentiment but through consistency.

RIGHTS THAT SUPPORT THE BALANCE

The U.S. Constitution provides several key rights that help maintain stability during encounters. The Fourth Amendment limits unreasonable searches and seizures. The Fifth Amendment protects against compelled self-incrimination. The Sixth Amendment guarantees the right to counsel after formal charges. These protections do not interfere with lawful policing; they guide it.

Citizens strengthen this balance by exercising their rights calmly and clearly. You may refuse consent to a search. You may remain silent beyond identification and required documents during traffic stops. You may ask whether you are free to leave. These actions are most effective when expressed without argument. Rights stated calmly are easier to respect, easier to document, and easier to evaluate later if needed.

RESPONSIBILITIES THAT SUPPORT THE BALANCE

Citizens hold responsibilities as well. Producing identification during a lawful traffic stop, following safety-based commands, and remaining in place during a detention are legal requirements. These obligations give officers space to perform their duties safely. They also reduce misunderstandings that can complicate or prolong the encounter.

Officers, in turn, have responsibilities shaped by case law and departmental procedure. They must follow the limits of reasonable suspicion, the rules governing probable cause, and the standards controlling searches. They must keep detentions limited to their lawful purpose and must document their actions accurately. Fulfilling these responsibilities creates the structure that protects citizen rights.

COMMUNICATION AS A PRACTICAL TOOL

Clear communication remains one of the most effective ways to keep an encounter steady. Citizens can support this by making statements concise and purposeful. Officers can support it by issuing direct instructions and providing explanations at appropriate moments.

Both sides benefit from avoiding assumptions. Citizens should not assume every instruction indicates suspicion. Officers should not assume every hesitation indicates defiance. When communication stays straightforward, errors decline. Predictable dialogue reduces uncertainty for everyone involved. Simple, measured exchanges also help clarify the purpose of each step. These habits make the encounter easier to manage on both sides.

SEEING THE ENCOUNTER AS A SHARED SPACE

Safe police encounters function best when both sides recognize that each has a role shaped by legal boundaries. Officers manage the scene, assess safety, and determine whether further action is required. Citizens assert their rights, provide required information, and maintain steady behavior. Neither role replaces the other. Instead, the two work together to create a predictable environment where constitutional protections remain intact.

Viewing the encounter as a shared space—rather than a contest—helps clarify what is happening. The officer's instructions organize the scene. Your rights organize your responses. The combination results in a controlled interaction that protects everyone involved. This approach keeps small misunderstandings from escalating. It also allows each side to perform its role without unnecessary tension. Over time these habits contribute to smoother encounters overall.

SUMMARY

Good citizenship and good policing depend on clear rights, clear responsibilities, and clear communication. Citizens protect themselves by exercising rights calmly and following lawful commands. Officers support safe encounters by applying constitutional standards consistently and providing structured guidance. When both sides understand their roles, police encounters become more predictable, more stable, and more respectful of the legal framework that governs them. This clarity helps prevent avoidable misunderstandings during brief roadside decisions. When both sides follow a consistent approach, the encounter stays safer and focused on its immediate purpose.

A healthy civic future rests on shared respect, clear expectations, and the steady partnership that grows between informed citizens and principled policing. Illustration copyright © Lochlainn Seabrook.

The End

APPENDICES

Police–citizen encounters follow well-defined constitutional rules, and understanding those rules is the key to staying safe, calm, and in control. Every situation—from a simple request for identification to an arrest—unfolds within a framework shaped by the Fourth, Fifth, and Sixth Amendments, state statutes, and long-established court decisions. Illustration copyright © Lochlainn Seabrook.

Appendix A

ORDER OF EVENTS DURING A TRAFFIC STOP

1. OFFICER OBSERVES VEHICLE

2. DECISION TO INITIATE STOP

3. EMERGENCY LIGHTS ACTIVATED

4. DRIVER PULLS OVER SAFELY

5. OFFICER APPROACHES DRIVER

6. INITIAL CONTACT & IDENTIFICATION

7. BRIEF QUESTIONING, IF NEEDED

8. SEARCH DECISION, IF NEEDED

9. RECORDS CHECK, CITATION DECISION, & CONCLUSION OF STOP

Though this aspect of policing is often ignored, officers routinely assist community members in moments that fall outside formal enforcement duties, reflecting the broader principle that police work includes caregiving responsibilities grounded in public safety. Illustration copyright © Lochlainn Seabrook.

Appendix B

WHAT YOU ARE LEGALLY REQUIRED TO DO DURING A TRAFFIC STOP

A Summary of Citizen Obligations Under U.S. Constitutional Law

Police encounters during traffic stops create only a narrow set of obligations for motorists. These obligations are limited, specific, and defined by Supreme Court rulings. Everything outside these requirements is generally protected by the Fourth and Fifth Amendments. The following summary outlines what drivers must do, what they may refuse, and the boundaries of lawful police authority.

WHAT YOU ARE REQUIRED TO DO

1. *Provide Required Driving Documents:*
When lawfully requested, a driver must present a valid driver's license, vehicle registration, and proof of insurance. These requirements are administrative conditions of operating a motor vehicle and do not violate the Fifth Amendment. Deliberate refusal may result in citation, arrest, or towing of the vehicle.

2. *Exit the Vehicle if Ordered:*
Under Pennsylvania v. Mimms (1977) and Maryland v. Wilson (1997), an officer may instruct a driver or passenger to exit the vehicle for safety reasons. No additional suspicion is required. While the person must comply, they retain all constitutional protections once outside, including the right to remain silent and the right to refuse searches.

3. *Provide Your Name in "Stop-and-Identify" States:*
Some states allow officers to require a detained person to state their name when the officer already has reasonable suspicion (Hiibel v. Sixth Judicial District Court, 2004). The requirement extends only to providing a name—not an address, explanation, or physical identification—unless individual state law demands otherwise. In states without such statutes even providing a name is generally optional.

WHAT YOU ARE NOT REQUIRED TO DO
Citizens retain all constitutional protections during a stop unless specific legal thresholds are satisfied. You do not have to:

• Answer questions about travel, destination, activities, or immigration status.
• Consent to searches of your vehicle, belongings, or person.

• Allow officers to view the contents of your phone.
• Participate in field sobriety tests in many jurisdictions (state laws vary).
• Provide explanations, apologies, or narratives.
• Incriminate yourself in any way.

Invoking these rights must be done calmly and without obstructing the officer's lawful duties.

ADDITIONAL NOTES FOR CLARITY

• *Passenger Obligations:* Passengers are generally required to remain at the scene while a stop is underway, as officers must maintain control of the encounter for safety reasons. An officer may request identification from a passenger at any time, but it becomes *mandatory* only when the officer has independent reasonable suspicion tied to that passenger or when state law imposes an ID requirement during detention. A passenger may ask, "Am I free to leave?" If the answer is yes, they may depart on foot unless the officer articulates a lawful reason to detain them further.
• *Duration of the Stop:* A traffic stop may last only as long as is reasonably necessary to complete its original mission—typically verifying documents, checking for warrants, and writing a citation. Prolonging the stop to investigate unrelated matters (such as drug inquiries) requires either consent, reasonable suspicion, or probable cause. Without one of these conditions, officers may not extend the stop simply to "look around" or engage in exploratory questioning.
• *Search Thresholds:* Officers must meet specific constitutional thresholds before conducting a search. A vehicle search requires probable cause, a clear safety justification (such as concern for weapons), or voluntary consent. Routine violations like speeding do not supply legal grounds for a search. Even when officers request consent, the citizen may decline politely. A refusal cannot be used as evidence of wrongdoing and does not provide grounds for a search.

SUMMARY

Mandatory Everywhere:
1. Provide requested driving documents—that is, driver's license, vehicle registration, and proof of insurance.
2. Exit the vehicle when lawfully ordered.
3. Provide your name—but only when state law requires it under a valid stop-and-identify statute.

All other actions are protected by the Fourth and Fifth Amendments. Individuals may remain silent, refuse searches, decline to answer questions, and otherwise rely on constitutional safeguards without penalty—provided they do not obstruct lawful police duties. This appendix offers a clear reference for understanding the limited scope of citizen obligations during traffic stops and the constitutional boundaries that protect individual rights.

Appendix C

WHY OFFICERS CAN ORDER YOU OUT OF A VEHICLE & HOW LAWFUL REMOVAL WORKS

Officers may instruct a driver or passenger to step out of a vehicle during any lawful traffic stop. This authority is supported by established constitutional doctrine that treats the request as a reasonable safety measure within the scope of a brief detention. The instruction does not require additional suspicion once the stop itself is valid.

Exit orders are used to maintain control of the encounter, reduce hazards associated with confined spaces, prevent access to hidden areas, and allow officers to separate occupants when needed. Courts have recognized that roadside encounters carry inherent risks, and that the temporary intrusion of stepping out is outweighed by those safety concerns.

Officers may give an exit order in the following situations:

- *During routine safety procedures in a lawful stop*: A valid traffic stop allows an officer to direct any occupant to exit without further suspicion.
- *When occupants must be separated for clarity*: Conflicting statements or uncertainty about roles may justify separating individuals.
- *When the officer observes behavior suggesting danger*: Movements toward hidden areas, attempts to conceal objects, or escalating tension can support an exit order.
- *Before a lawful vehicle search, inventory, or impoundment*: Occupants may be asked to step out so the officer can safely complete these tasks.
- *When a driver refuses to provide documents through the window*: If the stop cannot proceed safely through the opening provided, the officer may direct the driver to exit.
- *When the encounter has escalated into a detention or arrest*: Occupants may be removed as part of standard procedure for placing someone in custody.

Physical removal occurs only when a clear, lawful exit order is refused. Officers may use reasonable force to carry out the instruction, limited to the amount necessary to gain compliance. The law does not require an officer to leave a noncompliant individual inside a running vehicle during a detention.

In some encounters an occupant refuses to unlock the door, lower window, or comply with a clear exit order. When this happens, officers may escalate to methods that allow them to complete the detention safely. These steps follow the general rule that reasonable force may be used to enforce a lawful command.

If the doors remain locked and communication fails, *officers may break a side window to reach the interior lock. This is considered a controlled, targeted use of force and is used only when lesser options have been exhausted. Once the window is breached, officers may unlock the door, open it, and release the seatbelt to prevent injury during the removal.*

Physical extraction becomes the next step if the person still refuses to exit. Officers may guide the occupant out using arm-control techniques, body position, or leverage that minimizes harm while gaining compliance. If resistance increases, additional force options may be used, provided they remain proportionate and focused on safely concluding the encounter.

Officers may also reach into the vehicle to turn off the engine if the motorist resists with the car running. Disabling the vehicle prevents flight and reduces risk to the public and to officers standing beside the door. Removal may occur even when the driver remains seated and belted, and officers may unbuckle the belt to prevent restraint during extraction.

These measures are not limited to high-risk encounters. A standard traffic stop can escalate when a vehicle becomes a closed space officers cannot safely control. Courts have held that *officers are not required to accept the risks posed by a locked door, raised windows, or a running engine during a lawful detention.*

The same principles apply to passengers. A passenger may be removed if they refuse a lawful exit instruction or obstruct the stop. They may not be searched or further detained without additional grounds, but they may be physically removed when necessary to maintain safety.

Officers may also enter a vehicle when there is a reasonable belief of evidence destruction, imminent flight, or a medical emergency. Breaking a window to assist an unresponsive occupant, to stop a dangerous action, or to secure the vehicle is consistent with the duty to protect life and preserve safety during roadside encounters.

SUMMARY

A lawful traffic stop gives officers the authority to order any occupant out of the vehicle. If that order is refused, officers may use reasonable, proportionate force—including breaking a window, unlocking the door, releasing the seatbelt, and physically removing the person—to complete the detention safely. The guiding principle is constant: force may be used only to the degree necessary to enforce a lawful command and maintain control of the encounter. This authority does not permit punishment or retaliation; it is limited strictly to what is required for safety and compliance. Officers are trained to apply the minimum force needed and to end force as soon as control is achieved. For the citizen, the safest course is simple: *follow lawful instructions promptly and treat officers with respect.* Doing so reduces risk, prevents escalation, and helps conclude the encounter quickly and safely for everyone involved.

Appendix D

LANDMARK SUPREME COURT CASES AFFECTING POLICE-CITIZEN ENCOUNTERS (BY YEAR)

1. CARROLL V. UNITED STATES — 1925
This early ruling established the "automobile exception," allowing warrantless searches of vehicles when officers have probable cause that evidence or contraband is inside. Because vehicles are mobile and regulated, the Court determined that immediate searches may be necessary. Carroll forms the backbone of modern vehicle-search doctrine.

2. MIRANDA V. ARIZONA — 1966
Miranda requires officers to provide warnings before conducting custodial interrogations. These warnings inform individuals of their right to remain silent, their right to counsel, and the consequences of waiving those rights. Miranda is one of the most widely known legal protections and governs how questioning must be conducted after arrest.

3. KATZ V. UNITED STATES — 1967
Katz established that the Fourth Amendment protects people, not places, and introduced the modern expectation-of-privacy doctrine. Electronic monitoring of a phone booth was deemed a search even though no physical intrusion occurred. Katz underlies all modern privacy analyses and guides how courts evaluate what constitutes a "search."

4. TERRY V. OHIO — 1968
This case established the modern framework for investigative detentions. Officers may briefly stop an individual when they have reasonable suspicion—based on specific, articulable facts—that criminal activity may be occurring. If the officer reasonably believes the person may be armed, a limited frisk (a Terry stop) for weapons is permitted. Terry created the legal foundation for traffic-stop detentions, officer-safety measures, and the distinction between a brief stop and a full arrest.

5. CHIMEL V. CALIFORNIA — 1969

This ruling limits the scope of searches incident to arrest. Officers may search the person being arrested and the area within their immediate reach where a weapon or evidence could be accessed. Chimel prevents broader, room-wide searches during arrests and sets clear boundaries for protective sweeps during custodial actions.

6. SCHNECKLOTH V. BUSTAMONTE — 1973

The Court held that consent to search is valid even when the individual is not informed of their right to refuse. Consent must be voluntary, but officers are not required to give additional explanations. This case governs most roadside consent searches and clarifies what constitutes voluntary agreement.

7. PENNSYLVANIA V. MIMMS — 1977

The Court ruled that officers may order a driver out of a lawfully stopped vehicle as a standard safety practice. No additional suspicion is required, and the slight intrusion upon the driver is outweighed by officer-safety concerns. This decision is the central authority supporting exit orders during traffic stops and forms the basis for routine procedures used nationwide.

8. DELAWARE V. PROUSE — 1979

The Court held that random stops of vehicles without any suspicion are unconstitutional. Officers must have at least reasonable suspicion before stopping a motorist, unless the stop occurs within a lawful checkpoint program. This case protects citizens from arbitrary vehicle stops.

9. PAYTON V. NEW YORK — 1980

The Court held that warrantless entry into a home to make a routine felony arrest is unconstitutional. Absent exigent circumstances or consent, officers must obtain a warrant before crossing a private residence threshold. Payton remains a cornerstone case defining the sanctity of the home under the Fourth Amendment.

10. RHODE ISLAND V. INNIS — 1980

Innis defined "interrogation" as words or actions by officers that are reasonably likely to elicit an incriminating response. Routine conversation or neutral remarks do not qualify. This case clarifies when Miranda protections apply during police questioning.

11. NEW YORK V. BELTON — 1981

This case established the earlier rule that officers may search the passenger compartment of a vehicle incident to arrest. Although later limited by Arizona v. Gant, Belton remains an important part of vehicle-search history and explains how the law evolved. Including Belton gives citizens a clearer understanding of why Gant was necessary and how rules changed over time.

12. UNITED STATES V. ROSS — 1982
The Court ruled that when officers have probable cause to search a vehicle, they may search containers within it that could reasonably hold the item sought. Ross provides a clear rule about the scope of vehicle searches and reinforces the breadth of the automobile exception established in Carroll.

13. ILLINOIS V. GATES — 1983
Gates replaced the earlier rigid two-prong test for probable cause with a more flexible "totality of the circumstances" approach. This standard evaluates all available facts to determine whether probable cause exists. Gates is significant for officers, judges, and citizens because it defines how probable cause is assessed in everyday policing.

14. MICHIGAN V. LONG — 1983
This decision allows officers to conduct a limited protective search of a vehicle's passenger compartment when they reasonably believe a weapon may be present. Long extends Terry-style safety principles to the interior of vehicles and authorizes officers to check accessible areas where a weapon could be hidden.

15. BERKEMER V. MCCARTY — 1984
The Court clarified that ordinary traffic stops are detentions, not custodial arrests. Therefore, Miranda warnings are not required during roadside questioning unless the situation escalates into custody. This case helps define the line between a temporary stop and a custodial situation requiring warnings.

16. TENNESSEE V. GARNER — 1985
This case places strict limits on the use of deadly force. Deadly force may only be used to prevent the escape of a suspect who poses a significant threat of death or serious physical harm. Garner reshaped policies nationwide and remains the primary authority on the constitutional limits of lethal force.

17. GRAHAM V. CONNOR — 1989
Graham established the "objective reasonableness" standard for

evaluating police use of force. Courts assess force from the perspective of a reasonable officer on the scene, not with hindsight. Graham remains the controlling constitutional test for all force-related claims and governs how officer actions are evaluated.

18. MICHIGAN DEPT. OF STATE POLICE V. SITZ — 1990
The Court upheld the constitutionality of sobriety checkpoints. Brief stops to detect impaired driving were deemed reasonable due to the government's substantial interest in preventing drunk driving. Sitz outlines when checkpoints can be used and sets limits on their operation.

19. FLORIDA V. JIMENO — 1991
Jimeno determined that the scope of a consent search is defined by what a reasonable person would have understood from the officer's request. If a driver consents to a vehicle search for drugs, officers may open containers that could logically hold them. This case defines the practical limits of consent searches.

20. CALIFORNIA V. ACEVEDO — 1991
Acevedo clarified that officers may search a container within a vehicle when they have probable cause to believe the container holds contraband, even if they lack probable cause to search the entire vehicle. This ruling unified earlier, conflicting decisions and provides a straightforward rule for container searches in automobiles.

21. WHREN V. UNITED STATES — 1996
The Court ruled that if an officer has probable cause to believe a traffic violation occurred, the stop is lawful—even if the officer also had other motives. The key factor is the objective violation, not the officer's subjective intent. This is one of the most important traffic-stop cases in modern policing.

22. MARYLAND V. WILSON — 1997
Expanding on Mimms, this ruling confirms that officers may also order passengers out of a stopped vehicle for safety reasons. Passengers may be removed even when the original stop involves only the driver. This case clarifies that the safety concerns during traffic stops apply to all occupants, not just those suspected of traffic violations.

23. INDIANAPOLIS V. EDMOND — 2000
This decision ruled that drug-interdiction checkpoints are unconstitutional. While Sitz allowed DUI checkpoints, Edmond

clarified that checkpoints may not be used for general crime control. This case draws a clear boundary between permissible and impermissible roadblock purposes.

24. ATWATER V. LAGO VISTA — 2001
The Court held that officers may arrest a person for a minor traffic offense—even one punishable only by a fine—if the officer has probable cause. This case outlines the broad arrest authority available in minor-offense encounters.

25. UNITED STATES V. DRAYTON — 2002
In this case, the Court held that officers do not need to inform individuals of their right to refuse consent during voluntary encounters on buses or in public places. This decision reinforces principles from Schneckloth v. Bustamonte regarding consent searches.

26. UNITED STATES V. ARVIZU — 2002
This ruling reaffirmed the "totality of the circumstances" approach to reasonable suspicion. Officers may rely on the combined weight of many small factors to justify a stop, even if each factor alone seems minor. This case is frequently cited in modern reasonable-suspicion cases.

27. ILLINOIS V. CABALLES — 2005
The Court held that a drug-sniffing dog may be used during a traffic stop as long as the stop is not prolonged beyond the time needed to handle the traffic matter. This case pairs with Rodriguez v. United States and helps define the boundaries of using canine units.

28. BRENDLIN V. CALIFORNIA — 2007
This case held that passengers, not just drivers, are "seized" during traffic stops and therefore have standing to challenge the legality of the stop. This matters for passengers who may wish to contest evidence found during the encounter.

29. ARIZONA V. JOHNSON — 2009
The Court held that officers may frisk a passenger during a traffic stop if they have reasonable suspicion the person is armed and dangerous. The stop itself provides the lawful basis for the encounter, and Johnson outlines when officers may escalate to a protective pat-down. This case defines the limits of officer-safety searches involving passengers.

30. ARIZONA V. GANT — 2009

The Court limited vehicle searches incident to arrest. Officers may search a vehicle after arrest only if the arrestee could still access the passenger compartment or if there is reason to believe the vehicle contains evidence of the offense for which the arrest was made. Gant narrowed previous interpretations and reinforced constitutional limits on vehicle searches.

31. NAVARETTE V. CALIFORNIA — 2014

The Court ruled that a reliable 911 tip can provide reasonable suspicion for a traffic stop, even without direct officer observation of the violation. This case affects how anonymous information is evaluated in roadside encounters.

32. HEIEN V. NORTH CAROLINA — 2014

The Court ruled that a reasonable mistake of law by an officer can still justify a traffic stop. If an officer reasonably interprets a statute incorrectly, and the mistake is objectively understandable, the stop may still be valid. This case is crucial for explaining how lawful stops can arise even from unclear statutes.

33. RODRIGUEZ V. UNITED STATES — 2015

Rodriguez held that officers may not prolong a completed traffic stop—even by a brief period—without new reasonable suspicion. Tasks unrelated to the traffic violation cannot extend the duration of the stop. Rodriguez is one of the most important modern cases governing the length and scope of detentions.

SUMMARY

Taken together, these landmark decisions define the modern boundaries of police authority and citizen rights. They explain how stops begin, how searches are limited, how force is evaluated, and how evidence may be used in court. While the cases differ in scope, each one shapes how roadside encounters and criminal investigations work in daily life. Understanding these rulings helps citizens recognize what officers are permitted to do, what limits the U.S. Constitution imposes, and how lawful encounters should unfold.

These principles also clarify why certain commands are issued during a stop, why officers take specific safety measures, and how courts later judge those actions. By knowing the framework, motorists can better anticipate the flow of an encounter and avoid unnecessary escalation. As always, the safest and most responsible course for any motorist is to follow lawful instructions promptly and interact with officers with patience and respect.

Appendix E

THE FIRST AMENDMENT & POLICE ENCOUNTERS

The First Amendment protects a wide range of speech directed at government officials, including law enforcement. Citizens often assume that yelling, criticizing, or using profanity during a stop is illegal. In most situations, verbal expression alone is not a crime. This appendix explains what the First Amendment does and does not protect during encounters with police.

1. PROTECTED VERBAL EXPRESSION

Courts have consistently held that citizens may verbally challenge or criticize police without being arrested for the content of their words. This protection extends to speech that is loud, angry, disrespectful, or profane. In City of Houston v. Hill (1987), the U.S. Supreme Court stated that the First Amendment safeguards "a significant amount of verbal criticism and challenge directed at police officers." Speech, by itself, is protected even when it expresses frustration or opposition. Officers are expected to tolerate verbal objection unless it crosses into a legally recognized exception.

2. LIMITS ON PROTECTION

First Amendment protection ends when speech becomes conduct that interferes with an officer's lawful duties. Thus speech that obstructs or prevents an officer from performing required tasks is not protected. Examples include shouting so persistently that the officer cannot communicate instructions, interrupting an investigation, or refusing to comply with safety-related directions while continuing to argue.

Threats are also unprotected. A direct, credible statement of intent to harm an officer falls outside First Amendment protection. Courts recognize the "fighting words" doctrine—words likely to provoke an immediate violent reaction—though modern cases apply this exception rarely. These categories exist and remain part of the legal framework.

3. DISTINGUISHING SPEECH FROM OBSTRUCTION

The key distinction is between expression and interference. A citizen may object, complain, swear, or criticize without violating the law. What they may not do is hinder, delay, or obstruct the officer's ability to complete the stop. Failure to follow lawful instructions—such as remaining in the vehicle when ordered, providing identification when required, or stepping back for safety—can lead to lawful detention or arrest regardless of what is being said.

Many citizens believe that because their words are protected, they may continue speaking over the officer. Courts disagree. A person may speak freely, but must still allow the officer to perform required duties. Understanding this distinction helps prevent escalation.

4. PRACTICAL GUIDANCE FOR CITIZENS
Citizens should understand that verbal expression is largely protected, but it is wise to remain calm and controlled. Exercising speech rights while complying with lawful commands prevents conflict and protects both parties. A citizen may speak freely, but they must not interfere with the officer's performance of legal duties. Communicating objections clearly, complying with instructions, and addressing concerns afterward is the safest approach.

Citizens who record police encounters should follow instructions related to positioning and safety. Recording is protected, but standing too close, refusing to move, or physically interfering converts protected activity into obstruction.

5. WHY THIS APPENDIX MATTERS
Misunderstandings about First Amendment protection can lead to unnecessary conflict and legal consequences. Knowing the boundary between speech and obstruction helps citizens navigate encounters confidently and within the law.

The First Amendment protects what a person says; it does not protect behavior that disrupts a lawful police action. Clear knowledge of these limits reduces the risk of escalation and supports safer encounters for both citizens and officers.

These principles also help citizens evaluate their own conduct more accurately, avoid common misconceptions spread online, and recognize when a situation is moving from verbal disagreement into unlawful interference. Understanding these distinctions strengthens a citizen's ability to assert rights responsibly and lowers the likelihood of avoidable arrests.

Appendix F

THE FIFTH AMENDMENT INVOCATION RULE

The Fifth Amendment protects citizens from being compelled to incriminate themselves. Most people understand this right only in general terms. Popular culture has reinforced the idea that "remaining silent" is all that is required. In practice, the law draws a clear line between remaining silent and invoking the right to remain silent. This appendix explains that distinction so readers can avoid the common mistakes that have harmed many defendants.

1. WHY SILENCE ALONE IS NOT ENOUGH
Courts have held that *silence, by itself, does not automatically activate Fifth Amendment protection*. If a person chooses not to answer a question but does not explain why, that silence may be interpreted as ordinary behavior rather than a constitutional act. In some circumstances, prosecutors may point to unexplained silence as evidence of guilt or inconsistency.

The most cited example is Salinas v. Texas (2013). In that case, the suspect voluntarily answered police questions and then stopped. Because he had not clearly invoked his Fifth Amendment right, his silence was allowed into evidence. The Court ruled that the privilege must be *affirmatively claimed*.

2. WHEN SILENCE MAY BE USED AGAINST YOU
During non-custodial questioning—such as voluntary interviews, pre-arrest encounters, or casual conversations with police—*silence is not automatically protected. Without a clear invocation, courts may treat silence as any other behavior and allow prosecutors to comment on it.*

Even after someone is placed in custody, the same principle applies *until the individual expressly invokes the right to remain silent*. Remaining quiet without stating the reason may not be enough to prevent later use of that silence for impeachment purposes.

3. HOW TO PROPERLY INVOKE THE FIFTH AMENDMENT
To receive full constitutional protection, *a person must state that their silence is intentional and based on the Fifth Amendment*. Say the following to the officer in a calm, clear, audible voice:

"I am invoking my Fifth Amendment right and I do not wish to answer any questions."

No additional explanation is needed. Once invoked, the individual should remain respectful and consistent. If questioning continues, they should request legal counsel.

4. WHY THIS ISSUE CAUSES CONFUSION
Much of the confusion comes from television portrayals of police encounters. These portrayals often show people "staying quiet" without addressing the legal requirement of invocation. Miranda warnings add to the misunderstanding. Citizens assume that once told they "have the right to remain silent," they need only remain silent. In reality, courts have emphasized that the privilege must be claimed so that officers and later fact-finders understand the person's intent.

5. PRACTICAL GUIDANCE FOR CITIZENS
A citizen who chooses not to answer questions should do so politely and without argument. A simple, firm invocation provides clarity for both parties and reduces the risk of later misinterpretation.

Key points:
• Invoke the right expressly.
• Remain respectful throughout the encounter.
• Do not provide partial answers.

If questioned further, repeat the invocation or request counsel.

6. A NOTE ON LAW ENFORCEMENT
Officers operate within the legal rules established by the courts. Clear invocation removes ambiguity and helps officers proceed appropriately. Properly invoking rights benefits both parties by creating a defined boundary for the encounter.

7. WHY THIS APPENDIX MATTERS
This topic is rarely explained to the public, yet it affects the outcome of many cases. A citizen who believes silence alone is protective may unintentionally create legal problems that could have been avoided with a single spoken sentence. Understanding the invocation rule strengthens the individual's ability to navigate police encounters safely and lawfully. It clarifies when rights are active and how a simple misstep can influence what evidence is later considered, helping ensure that a citizen's intentions are fully understood.

Appendix G

WHY YOU SHOULD NEVER CONSENT TO A VEHICLE SEARCH

Even if you believe you have done nothing wrong, it is rarely wise to consent to a vehicle search. A search conducted with your permission bypasses important Fourth Amendment protections and eliminates your ability to challenge the search later. Officers do not need your consent when the law already gives them independent authority to search. When they ask for permission, it often means they do not yet have the legal grounds to proceed without it.

A common misunderstanding is that "if I'm innocent, I have nothing to hide." In practice, innocence does not prevent complications. Vehicles often contain items that can be misinterpreted, such as tools, containers, prescription bottles, or belongings left by previous owners or passengers. Even a harmless object can raise suspicion if viewed out of context. Consent allows officers to examine these items without limitation, increasing the potential for confusion and unnecessary escalation.

You cannot predict how an officer will interpret what is found inside your vehicle. Something you view as ordinary may be seen as evidence of contraband or linked to criminal activity. Consent also allows the officer to search more thoroughly than many citizens realize. Once permission is granted, an officer may inspect compartments, bags, and containers if they believe the inspection is reasonably related to the search. You may withdraw consent—unless officers have already developed independent probable cause, at which point the search will continue without it.

Refusing consent does not signal guilt. The Supreme Court has made clear that declining consent is a protected choice and cannot be used as evidence of wrongdoing. You may refuse politely by saying, "I do not consent to searches." This statement preserves your rights while keeping the interaction respectful and controlled. Officers who already have probable cause or other lawful authority will conduct the search regardless, meaning your refusal only prevents searches that rely on your permission.

Another risk of consenting to a vehicle search arises from the possibility that unknown items may be in your vehicle. Many drivers have sold or purchased used vehicles, given rides to others, transported equipment, or carried items long forgotten in storage compartments. Something as small as a spent cartridge, a pocketknife, or a flake of plant material can become the focus of a search. By withholding consent, you ensure that only searches supported by law are carried out.

Understanding the difference between cooperation and consent is essential. Cooperation means following lawful commands, providing identification when required, and communicating respectfully. Consent is a voluntary waiver of constitutional protection. You can cooperate fully without granting permission to search. Officers are trained to respect a clear refusal to consent, and most will simply continue with the lawful steps of the stop.

If an officer requests permission to search your vehicle, you may decline without hostility. A calm and direct response such as "I do not consent to any searches" is sufficient. This preserves your rights, prevents misunderstandings, and ensures that any search that does occur must meet the legal standards required by the Fourth Amendment. Remaining consistent in your communication protects both you and the integrity of any future legal process.

Officers may also request consent as a way to resolve uncertainty during a stop. A driver who agrees to a search provides officers with additional information at the cost of personal privacy. A driver who declines consent maintains a clearer boundary around the interaction. Refusal does not impede legitimate investigative steps; it simply requires officers to rely on lawful standards rather than voluntary permission. This distinction matters, because consent-based searches are among the most commonly litigated areas of Fourth Amendment law. The cleanest approach for citizens is to avoid creating ambiguity.

Another practical consideration is the scope of the search. When you consent, the scope is determined by what an officer reasonably believes you allowed. Courts often interpret consent broadly, permitting officers to inspect any area where the object of the search might logically be found. This can include locked containers, bags, luggage, tools, and interior compartments. Most drivers do not anticipate how extensive a consent search may become. By refusing consent, you keep that scope defined by objective legal standards, not by broad assumptions about what you "must have meant."

Consent also alters the way evidence is treated in court. Evidence discovered during a lawful but warrantless search can sometimes be challenged if the search exceeded legal justification. Evidence discovered after voluntary consent is much more difficult to dispute. Courts will generally uphold what you agreed to. Declining consent preserves your ability to challenge questionable findings later and ensures that any dispute focuses on the officer's justification, not on a decision made under pressure.

Finally, declining consent promotes predictability and clarity for everyone involved. It signals that you understand the boundary between cooperation and waiver of rights. It keeps the encounter structured around established procedures rather than voluntary intrusions. Most importantly, it removes the possibility that a misunderstanding or misinterpretation during a high-stress stop will lead to unnecessary legal complications. A simple, respectful refusal—"I do not consent to searches"—remains one of the strongest and most effective tools available to citizens during roadside encounters.

Appendix H

MISDEMEANORS & FELONIES
EXPLAINED & DEFINED

MISDEMEANOR
A misdemeanor is a criminal offense considered less serious than a felony. It typically involves conduct that causes limited harm, low financial loss, or minor risk to others. Misdemeanors are generally handled in lower courts and rarely result in long-term incarceration.

Typical Penalties (penalties vary by state, but these ranges are consistent nationwide):

• Jail: Up to 1 year in a county or municipal jail (many states cap at 6 months).
• Fines: Commonly $100 to $5,000, depending on the offense.
• Probation: Often 6 months to 3 years.
• Additional sanctions: Community service, classes (e.g., anger management, DUI education), no-contact orders, license suspensions, restitution.

Most first-time misdemeanor defendants receive probation, fines, or diversion programs instead of jail time.

INFRACTION / VIOLATION
An infraction (sometimes called a violation) is the lowest category of unlawful conduct. It includes non-criminal offenses such as most traffic citations, ordinance violations, and other minor regulatory breaches. Infractions do not carry jail time.

Typical Penalties:
• Fines: Usually $25 to $500, depending on the violation.
• Additional sanctions: Traffic school, safety classes, or remedial courses.
• Criminal record: Infractions are generally not considered criminal convictions and rarely appear on standard background checks.

FELONY

A felony is a serious criminal offense that involves significant harm, high-value loss, the use of force or weapons, or conduct that poses substantial danger to others. Felony cases are handled in higher courts, carry longer sentences, and have longer-lasting legal consequences.

Typical Penalties (every state divides felonies into classes, but the ranges below reflect the national norms):

Prison:
- Low-level felonies: 1 to 3 years.
- Mid-level felonies: 3 to 7 years.
- High-level felonies: 10 to 25 years.
- Most serious felonies: 25 years to life (or, in some states, life without parole).

- Fines: Often $5,000 to $100,000+, depending on degree and state law.
- Probation: In some cases, 1 to 5 years, usually for lower-grade felonies.
- Additional sanctions: Parole, mandatory supervision, firearm prohibitions, restitution, mandatory treatment programs.

A felony conviction typically affects civil rights (firearms restrictions, voting rights in some states) and may impact employment and licensing.

COLLATERAL CONSEQUENCES

Criminal convictions can create effects beyond the formal sentence. These consequences vary by jurisdiction and by the nature of the offense. Common areas affected:

- Employment: Some occupations restrict applicants with recent convictions.
- Licenses: Professional or occupational boards may review criminal histories.
- Firearms: Federal law prohibits firearm possession after certain convictions.
- Immigration: Non-citizens may face additional review or consequences.
- Driving privileges: DUI-related cases often include license suspensions.

These consequences are not part of the judge's sentence but stem from other laws or regulatory agencies.

HOW STATES CLASSIFY CRIMINAL OFFENSES
States organize criminal offenses into structured categories to define sentencing ranges, guide court procedures, and maintain consistency across cases. Though terminology differs from state to state, every system serves the same basic purpose: to group crimes by seriousness and apply proportionate penalties. Below are the major approaches used nationwide, expanded for clarity.

CLASS SYSTEM
Many states classify both misdemeanors and felonies into lettered tiers, A, B, C, D:

Class A: The most serious level within each category. Class A misdemeanors often allow jail terms up to the statutory maximum for misdemeanors, while Class A felonies carry the longest prison ranges, highest fines, and the strictest collateral consequences.

Class B: One tier below Class A. Penalties are significant but reduced. Class B misdemeanors may involve short jail terms or conditional sentences; Class B felonies carry substantial prison exposure but less than Class A.

Class C: Mid-range offenses. Class C misdemeanors may involve fines or brief detention; Class C felonies typically include shorter prison terms, limited fines, and increased use of probation.

Class D: Lower-level offenses. Class D misdemeanors often carry minimal jail exposure and smaller fines. Class D felonies sit at the bottom of the felony range and may include alternative sentencing options or short prison terms.

DEGREE SYSTEM
Common in offenses involving violence, sexual conduct, and major property crimes, 1st–4th Degree:

First Degree: Reserved for the most serious conduct, often involving intentional harm, deadly weapons, or significant injury. Penalties can include long prison terms or mandatory minimums.

Second Degree: Serious but without the aggravating elements of first-degree charges. Often used when harm or risk is high but less extreme.

Third Degree: Mid-level offenses involving lower harm, lesser intent, or reduced danger. Penalties vary widely.

Fourth Degree: Lower-tier crimes that still fall within the structured degree system but carry shorter sentences and fewer mandatory enhancements.

LEVEL SYSTEM (1–6)

Used in states that have replaced older class or degree structures.

Level 1: Most serious. Long prison terms, higher fines, and enhanced sentencing rules.

Levels 2–3: Serious but below Level 1. Often used for major property or injury-related offenses.

Level 4: Mid-range. Includes conduct that is harmful or risky but not severe enough for a higher level.

Levels 5–6: Least serious within the system. Often eligible for probation, diversion, or suspended sentences.

UNCLASSIFIED OFFENSES

Some crimes do not fit into standard class, degree, or level systems. These are given their own statutory penalties. Examples include certain regulatory offenses, unique state-specific crimes, or rarely prosecuted statutory offenses. Penalties are set individually by statute rather than by category.

VALUE-BASED CLASSIFICATIONS

Used primarily in theft, fraud, property damage, and financial-loss cases. The seriousness of the charge rises as the value of the loss increases. Higher value can elevate a misdemeanor to a felony or raise a felony from a lower tier to a higher one. This system links punishment to measurable economic harm.

HARM-BASED CLASSIFICATIONS

Some states scale charges based on the degree of physical injury, risk to children, threat to public safety, or danger posed to emergency responders. More serious harm or greater risk elevates the charge, increases penalties, and may trigger mandatory minimums or enhanced sentencing rules.

INTENT-BASED CLASSIFICATIONS

Many criminal statutes distinguish between purposeful, knowing, reckless, and negligent conduct. Offenses requiring higher intent—such as purposeful or knowing action—are punished more severely than those involving mere negligence. This system ties the penalty to the defendant's mental state rather than the outcome alone.

WHY CRIMINAL CLASSIFICATION MATTERS

- *Sets sentencing boundaries*: Defines the maximum and minimum punishment allowed by law for each offense.
- *Guides judicial decisions*: Helps judges apply statewide sentencing rules, determine probation eligibility, and structure suspended or conditional sentences.
- *Shapes plea negotiations*: Provides defendants and attorneys with a clear sense of likely outcomes, aiding realistic case evaluation.
- *Promotes fairness*: Ensures similar cases receive similar treatment, improving statewide consistency and reducing arbitrary disparities.
- *Reflects legislative priorities*: Allows lawmakers to rank offenses by intent, harm, risk, or public-policy concerns, keeping penalties aligned with current standards.
- *Gives citizens clarity*: Offers an understandable framework for assessing the potential consequences of a charge and distinguishing between minor and serious offenses.

Police officers are not defined solely by enforcement duties; they also serve as everyday helpers, guides, and problem-solvers for the public. Scenes like this highlight the human side of policing—simple acts of assistance, moments of connection, and a willingness to help those in need—all of which strengthen trust, understanding, and community confidence. Illustration copyright © Lochlainn Seabrook.

Appendix I

STATE & FEDERAL CHARGES EXPLAINED & DEFINED

OVERVIEW
Criminal charges in the United States fall into two main systems: *state* and *federal*. Most crimes are handled by state or local authorities, but certain offenses fall under federal jurisdiction. The distinction affects who investigates, who prosecutes, where the case is heard, and what penalties apply.

WHEN A CRIME BECOMES A FEDERAL OFFENSE
A crime is typically charged federally when it:
• crosses state lines.
• involves federal land or federal property.
• involves federal agencies or federal personnel.
• violates a federal statute.
• affects interstate commerce.
• involves immigration, customs, or border issues.
• relates to national security or federal programs.

If a crime does not meet one of these conditions, it is almost always charged at the state level.

WHO INVESTIGATES STATE CHARGES
• Local police departments.
• County sheriffs.
• State police / highway patrol.
• Local detectives or investigators.

WHO INVESTIGATES FEDERAL CHARGES
• FBI.
• DEA.
• ATF.
• U.S. Secret Service.
• Homeland Security Investigations.
• U.S. Marshals.
• Postal Inspection Service.
• Other federal task forces.

WHO PROSECUTES STATE CHARGES
• Elected District Attorneys (DAs).
• County prosecutors.
• State attorneys.

WHO PROSECUTES FEDERAL CHARGES
• U.S. Attorneys, appointed by the Department of Justice.

Federal prosecutors handle far fewer cases overall, but the cases they choose to file tend to be stronger, more complex, and supported by longer investigations.

WHERE THE CASE IS TRIED
State Charges:
• State courts.
• City or county courts.
• Local judges and juries.
Federal Charges:
• U.S. District Court.
• Federal judges appointed for life.
• Federal juries.

Appeals go to federal appellate courts and potentially to the Supreme Court.

PENALTIES & SENTENCING
State Charges: Penalties vary widely by state, but generally include
• county jail time (misdemeanors).
• state prison time (felonies).
• probation.
• fines.
• community service.
• treatment programs.

Sentencing is based on state law and local guidelines.

Federal Charges: Federal cases often carry
• longer prison sentences.
• mandatory minimums for certain offenses.
• no parole (sentence must be served; supervision follows release).
• higher fines.
• federal restitution requirements.

Sentencing follows the Federal Sentencing Guidelines.

EXAMPLES OF STATE CHARGES
• DUI.
• simple assault.
• burglary.
• domestic violence.
• petty theft.
• most drug possession cases.
• most traffic misdemeanors.

EXAMPLES OF FEDERAL CHARGES
• drug trafficking across state lines.
• wire fraud and mail fraud.
• bank robbery (FDIC-insured banks).
• firearms violations involving federal law.
• crimes on military bases, national parks, or federal buildings.
• immigration-related offenses.
• child exploitation involving interstate digital/internet activity.

TAKEAWAY
Most citizens will only encounter state charges, not federal ones. Federal cases are less common, more complex, and usually involve broader criminal conduct or violations of federal statutes. Although state and federal systems operate separately, they often work together. A case may start with local police, shift to a federal agency, or be jointly handled through a task force when the conduct reaches both jurisdictions. Prosecutors decide which system moves forward based on the evidence, the elements of the offense, and the scope of the investigation.

Federal agencies have broader resources, specialized units, and national reach, enabling long-term or multi-state cases. State and local authorities focus on offenses affecting their communities, emphasizing rapid response and public safety. This division of labor means most crimes stay local, while federal agencies handle matters requiring wider authority. These structural differences explain why some offenses remain in state court while others move to federal court, and why penalties can differ sharply depending on who brings the charge.

Federal agencies may also approach the same conduct differently, focusing on broader patterns or multi-state activity. State authorities tend to prioritize immediate community impact, creating distinct outcomes for similar behavior.

An arrest can enter either the state or federal system, with each path shaping what follows—from who investigates the case to how it is ultimately charged and sentenced. The girl being taken into custody here represents the starting point of a process in which jurisdiction, agency involvement, and statutory authority determine the route a case may take. Illustration copyright © Lochlainn Seabrook.

Appendix J

COMMON CRIMES & THEIR DEFINITIONS
(ALPHABETIZED & CLASSIFIED)

KEY
M: Usually charged as a misdemeanor.
F: Usually charged as a felony.
M/F: Can be either depending on severity, value, injury, weapon, or state law.

Abandoning a Child (F): Leaving a child without supervision under dangerous conditions.

Abuse of a Corpse (M/F): Improper handling, concealment, or desecration of a human body.

Accessory After the Fact (F): Assisting an offender to avoid arrest or prosecution.

Accessory Before the Fact (F): Helping plan or enable a crime.

Aggravated Assault (F): Assault involving serious injury or a deadly weapon.

Aggravated Battery (F): Battery causing severe injury or involving a weapon.

Aggravated Burglary (F): Burglary while armed or causing injury.

Aggravated DUI (F): DUI with injury, death, or repeat offenses.

Aggravated Identity Theft (F): Identity theft with aggravating factors such as minors or financial losses.

Aggravated Robbery (F): Robbery with a weapon or injury.

Aiding and Abetting (F): Intentionally helping another commit a crime.

Animal Cruelty (M/F): Inflicting pain on or neglecting an animal.

Animal Fighting (F): Organizing or participating in animal fighting.

Arson (F): Intentionally setting fire to property or land.

Arson of a Dwelling (F): Burning a home or occupied structure.

Assault (Simple) (M): Causing reasonable fear of immediate harm.

Attempted Murder (F): Attempting to kill another person.

Attempted Theft (M/F): Attempting to unlawfully take property.

Battery (Simple) (M): Unlawful physical contact causing minor injury.

Bestiality (F): Engaging in sexual acts with an animal.

Blackmail (F): Obtaining something through threats.

Bomb Possession (F): Possessing or manufacturing explosive devices.

Bomb Threat (F): Threatening to use an explosive.

Bribery (F): Offering or accepting value to influence official action.

Burglary (F): Entering a structure to commit a crime.

Burglary of a Vehicle (M/F): Unlawful entry into a vehicle.

Carjacking (F): Taking a vehicle by force or intimidation.

Carrying a Concealed Weapon Illegally (M/F): Concealed carry contrary to state law.

Check Fraud (M/F): Passing or creating fraudulent checks.

Child Abuse (F): Causing physical, emotional, or sexual harm to a child.

Child Endangerment (M/F): Putting a child in a harmful situation.

Child Exploitation (F): Using a child for sexual or labor-related purposes.

Child Molestation (F): Sexual conduct with a minor.

Child Neglect (M/F): Failure to provide adequate care or supervision.

Commercial Burglary (F): Burglary of a business.

Computer Intrusion (M/F): Unauthorized access to computers or networks.

Concealing Identity (M): Hiding identity during a crime.

Conspiracy (F): Agreement to commit a felony.

Contempt of Court (M/F): Disobeying a lawful court order.

Contributing to the Delinquency of a Minor (M/F): Encouraging illegal acts by a minor.

Credit Card Fraud (F): Using someone's card or data to obtain goods or money.

Criminal Coercion (M/F): Using threats to compel action.

Criminal Impersonation (M/F): Pretending to be another person for gain.

Criminal Mischief (M/F): Damaging or tampering with property.

Criminal Negligence (M/F): Failure to exercise reasonable care causing harm.

Criminal Simulation (M/F): Creating or altering objects to defraud.

Criminal Trespass (M): Entering property without legal permission, or remaining after permission has been revoked.

Cultivation of Controlled Substances (F): Growing illegal drugs.

Cyber Harassment (M): Electronic harassment without threats.

Cyberstalking (M/F): Online threats or persistent unwanted contact.

Dating Violence (M/F): Abuse within a dating relationship.

Defacing Property (M): Damaging or marking property unlawfully.

Defrauding an Innkeeper (M/F): Obtaining lodging or services without payment.

Deprivation of Rights Under Color of Law (F): Illegal denial of constitutional rights by an official.

Desecration (M/F): Damaging cemeteries, gravestones, statues, memorials, or sacred items.

Disarming a Peace Officer (F): Taking or attempting to take an officer's weapon.

Disorderly Conduct (M): Disturbing public order or peace.

Disturbing the Peace (M): Behavior disrupting public tranquility.

Domestic Battery (M/F): Physical harm in a domestic setting.

Domestic Violence (M/F): Assault or threats in a household relationship.

Drug Manufacturing (F): Producing controlled substances.

Drug Paraphernalia Possession (M): Possessing equipment for drug use.

Drug Possession (M/F): Unauthorized possession of illegal drugs.

Drug Trafficking / Distribution (F): Selling or transporting illegal drugs.

DUI / DWI (M/F): Driving under the influence of alcohol or drugs. May be charged as a misdemeanor or felony depending on prior convictions, injury or death, presence of minors, BAC level, or other aggravating factors.

Eavesdropping (M/F): Illegally recording or listening to private communications.

Elder Abuse (F): Harm or neglect of an elderly person.

Embezzlement (M/F): Taking property entrusted to one's care.

Escape (F): Fleeing custody or confinement.

Excessive Speeding (M): Driving significantly above the legal limit.

Exhibition of Speed (M): Racing or accelerating dangerously.

Exploitation of the Elderly (F): Financial or physical abuse of an elderly person.

Extortion (F): Using threats to obtain money or actions.

Failing to Appear (M/F): Failure to appear for court.

Failing to Obey a Lawful Order (M): Refusing lawful commands by police.

False Imprisonment (F): Unlawful restraint of a person.

False Information to Police (M): Knowingly giving false details.

False Reporting (M): Making a false police report.

Financial Fraud (F): Deception for financial gain.

Firearms Violations (General) (M/F): Illegal possession or use of firearms.

Fleeing and Eluding (M/F): Fleeing a lawful traffic stop or police pursuit.

Forgery (F): Creating or using false documents.

Fraud (General) (F): Deception for unlawful gain.

Gambling Violation (M): Illegal gambling.

Grand Larceny (F): Theft above the state's felony threshold.

Harassment (M): Conduct intended to annoy or alarm.

Hate Crime (F): Crime motivated by legal bias categories.

Hazing (M/F): Initiation causing risk of harm.

Hindering Prosecution (F): Assisting someone to avoid arrest or conviction.

Hit-and-Run (M/F): Leaving an accident scene unlawfully.

Homicide (Criminal) (F): Unlawfully causing another's death.

Identity Theft (F): Using another's personal information without permission.

Illegal Dumping (M): Unlawful disposal of waste.

Illegal Gambling Operation (F): Operating an unauthorized gambling business.

Illegal Possession of Ammunition (M/F): Holding ammunition unlawfully.

Illegal Possession of a Firearm (F): Possession of a firearm by a prohibited person.

Illegal Surveillance (M/F): Monitoring others without consent.

Impersonating a Public Official (F): Pretending to hold government authority.

Indecent Exposure (M/F): Intentional lewd exposure of genitals.

Insurance Fraud (F): False claims to obtain insurance benefits.

Interfering With an Officer (M/F): Obstructing lawful police actions.

Intimidation (M/F): Threats intended to influence or scare another.

Kidnapping (F): Unlawfully confining or transporting a person.

Larceny (M/F): Unlawful taking of property.

Leaving the Scene of an Accident (M/F): Failure to stop or provide details.

Lewd Conduct (M/F): Sexual or obscene behavior in public.

Loitering (M): Remaining in place without lawful purpose after being told to leave.

Mail Fraud (F): Using mail systems to defraud.

Mail Theft (F): Stealing or tampering with mail.

Making Terroristic Threats (F): Threats intended to cause fear or disruption.

Manslaughter (Voluntary) (F): Killing under sudden provocation.

Manslaughter (Involuntary) (F): Killing through reckless or negligent acts.

Menacing (M/F): Threatening injury or harm.

Misapplication of Fiduciary Property (M/F): Misusing property entrusted to one's care.

Misuse of 911 (M): Knowingly using emergency services for non-emergency purposes, including false or disruptive calls.

Money Laundering (F): Concealing the source of illegal funds.

Mortgage Fraud (F): Fraud in obtaining loans or property.

Motor Vehicle Theft (F): Stealing or attempting to steal a vehicle.

Murder (First Degree) (F): Premeditated unlawful killing.

Murder (Second Degree) (F): Intentional killing without premeditation.

Negligent Homicide (F): Causing death through negligence.

Obstruction of Justice (M/F): Interfering with investigations or court proceedings.

Open Container Violation (M): Open alcohol in a vehicle or restricted area.

Perjury (F): Lying under oath.

Petty Theft (M): Low-value theft.

Possession of Burglary Tools (F): Holding tools intended for unlawful entry.

Possession of Child Pornography (F): Possessing exploitative images of minors.

Possession of Controlled Substances (M/F): Illegal possession of drugs.

Possession of Stolen Property (M/F): Possessing property known to be stolen.

Possession of a Weapon in Prohibited Area (M/F): Weapon possession where banned.

Prostitution (M): Exchanging sexual acts for money.

Public Intoxication (M): Being dangerously intoxicated in public.

Rape (F): Non-consensual sexual intercourse.

Reckless Driving (M/F): Driving with wilful disregard for safety.

Reckless Endangerment (M/F): Conduct risking serious injury.

Receiving Stolen Property (M/F): Accepting property known to be stolen.

Resisting Arrest (M/F): Obstructing or fleeing lawful arrest.

Retail Fraud / Shoplifting (M/F): Theft from a store.

Robbery (F): Taking property by force or threat.

Sabotage (F): Deliberately damaging property or operations.

Sexual Assault (F): Non-consensual sexual contact.

Sexual Battery (F): Non-consensual sexual touching.

Sexual Exploitation of a Minor (F): Using a minor sexually.

Simple Possession of Ammunition by Minor (M): Minor possessing ammunition unlawfully.

Solicitation (M/F): Encouraging or requesting a crime.

Speeding in a School Zone (M): Exceeding the posted speed limit in a designated school zone.

Stalking (M/F): Repeated contact causing fear.

Statutory Rape (F): Sexual activity with a minor below consent age.

Tax Evasion (F): Avoiding lawful taxes.

Terrorism (State-Level) (F): Acts meant to intimidate or coerce a population.

Theft by Deception (M/F): Obtaining property through deception.

Theft by Receiving (M/F): Receiving property known to be stolen.

Threatening a Public Official (F): Threats to intimidate an official.

Unauthorized Practice of a Profession (M/F): Performing regulated services without a license.

Unauthorized Use of a Vehicle (M/F): Using a vehicle without permission.

Unlawful Assembly (M): Gathering to commit a crime.

Unlawful Imprisonment (F): Restricting someone's movement without consent.

Unlawful Surveillance (M/F): Recording or observing someone without permission.

Unlawful Weapon Possession (M/F): Illegal possession of a weapon.

Vandalism (M/F): Damaging or defacing property.

Vehicular Homicide (F): Causing death through unlawful or reckless driving.

Voyeurism (M/F): Secretly observing for sexual purposes.

Welfare Fraud (F): Fraudulently obtaining public benefits.

Wire Fraud (F): Using communication systems to defraud.

Witness Intimidation (F): Attempting to influence or scare a witness.

The United States is a nation of laws where actions carry consequences.
Illustration copyright © Lochlainn Seabrook.

Appendix K

COMMON PSEUDO-LEGAL MYTHS ABOUT POLICE STOPS

Some citizens encounter misleading legal claims online that promise to invalidate police authority during a traffic stop or other encounter. These ideas often appear in videos, forums, and prewritten "scripts." Due to the false information they contain, they can create unsafe, even potentially deadly, situations for both drivers and officers. This appendix separates fact from fiction by outlining the most common pseudo-legal assertions and explaining their actual legal status.

THE "SOVEREIGN CITIZEN" MISUNDERSTANDING
A small but visible group of individuals believe they are exempt from federal or state law based on personal interpretations of the Constitution, common law, or historical terms. Going by the name "sovereign citizens," they may assert that they do not "consent" to government authority, that only certain courts have jurisdiction over them, or that they are not required to hold a driver's license. These claims have no basis in American law and are rejected by every U.S. court. Officers are trained to be aware of these statements: they can signal misunderstanding of legal obligations or, in some cases, refusal to comply.

"I DO NOT CONSENT" SCRIPTS
Some online sources provide memorized lines intended to prevent lawful identification requests, citations, or arrests. In fact, citizens may refuse consent to a search, but they cannot prevent an officer from acting when the law authorizes it. Using scripted lines does not create legal protection and can complicate or escalate the encounter.

JURISDICTION MYTHS
Another common claim is that an officer lacks jurisdiction unless the driver verbally accepts it. In reality, a police officer's authority is established by state law and does not depend on individual consent. When an officer has legal cause to initiate a stop, jurisdiction already exists. Courts have repeatedly held that jurisdiction cannot be avoided through special wording, alternative identification, or fake license plates.

DRIVER VS. TRAVELER CLAIMS
Some individuals argue that they are "travelers" (traveling) not "drivers" (driving) and therefore exempt from licensing and registration rules. *All states define the operation of a motor vehicle as a regulated activity requiring a*

license, regardless of terminology. Personal beliefs about wording do not override motor-vehicle law.

FALSE FILINGS & PAPERWORK TACTICS
Another pseudo-legal strategy involves filing homemade liens, unofficial notices, or documents intended to nullify a citation or arrest. These documents have no legal effect and may result in civil or criminal penalties. Courts treat such tactics as fraudulent or frivolous filings, not as valid legal remedies.

WHY COURTS REJECT THESE ARGUMENTS
Judges at all levels, including federal appellate courts, have rejected the claims listed above. Courts consistently rule that *individual interpretations of constitutional or historical text cannot supersede established statutory law.* Because these arguments fail in every setting, citizens should avoid relying on them.

HOW TO AVOID BAD ONLINE ADVICE
Citizens sometimes adopt pseudo-legal claims after encountering inaccurate legal advice online (primarily social media). The safest approach is straightforward: follow lawful instructions, stay calm, and rely on recognized constitutional protections. Asking clear questions is appropriate; confrontational or scripted phrases are not.

PRACTICAL NOTE FOR CITIZENS
Officers may use additional caution if a "sov cit" driver repeats these statements, because they are trained to recognize them during traffic stops. This does not mean the officer is treating the driver as a threat. It reflects awareness that misunderstandings can escalate an encounter. As always, clear communication protects both parties.

FINAL GUIDANCE
Citizens do not need special wording to preserve their rights. Established constitutional standards already protect them. Claims that promise to "invalidate" a stop or cancel an officer's authority have no legal foundation. Polite cooperation, respectful compliance, and accurate knowledge remain the most effective tools during any police encounter.

NOTE: At this time there is no official police radio code for identifying sovereign-citizen behavior. Agencies rely on plain-language descriptions or internal dispatch notes rather than numeric codes. As these encounters continue to rise in various jurisdictions—unfortunately often involving refusal to comply, obstruction, resisting, or other confrontational behavior—it is possible that a standardized classification may eventually be adopted to help officers recognize and communicate "sov cit" situations more efficiently.

Appendix L

COMMON MYTHS ABOUT POLICE WORK

The public often holds assumptions about how police agencies operate internally. While these particular misconceptions concern pay structures, incentives, staffing, and administrative rules, such myths can and do affect the public's encounters with police.

Myth 1. *Police have daily or monthly quota requirements for citations and arrests.* Reality: Departments operate on merit, with most prohibiting quotas; performance is based on overall conduct, documentation quality, and responsiveness rather than numbers.

Myth 2. *Police get paid extra for each arrest they make.* Reality: Arrests provide no additional income; compensation is fixed by salary schedules, contracts, and overtime rules.

Myth 3. *Officers receive bonuses for writing more citations.* Reality: No department compensates per citation; citation activity is monitored for accuracy and lawfulness, not volume.

Myth 4. *Departments reward officers financially for generating revenue.* Reality: Police budgets are not tied to individual officer output; revenue from fines is handled through separate municipal or state processes.

Myth 5. *Officers keep a portion of fines, seized property, or forfeiture funds.* Reality: Officers have no personal access to these funds; forfeiture and fine revenue is controlled by courts and government finance offices.

Myth 6. *Police overtime is unlimited and unregulated.* Reality: Overtime is capped by department policy, union agreements, and staffing needs; officers must obtain supervisory approval.

Myth 7. *Officers lose pay when they issue warnings instead of citations.* Reality: Pay is not influenced by enforcement choices; warnings are part of normal discretionary policing.

Myth 8. *Supervisors punish officers who do not meet certain arrest numbers.* Reality: Officers are evaluated on professionalism, report quality, judgment, and community interaction rather than numerical targets.

Myth 9. *Departments evaluate officers primarily on how many arrests they make.* Reality: Arrest totals play a small role in work documentation and are never the sole measure of performance.

Myth 10. *Officer performance reviews are tied to revenue generation.*

Reality: Financial outcomes are not considered in reviews; performance focuses on adherence to policy, safety, and lawful conduct.

Myth 11. *Police departments hire almost anyone who applies.* Reality: Hiring requires background checks, psychological screening, physical testing, and interviews, with most applicants not reaching final selection.

Myth 12. *Agencies bypass background checks when they are understaffed.* Reality: Background investigations are mandatory; staffing shortages do not override state and departmental hiring requirements.

Myth 13. *Academy training lasts only a few weeks with minimal standards.* Reality: State academies require months of instruction and testing, covering law, defensive tactics, emergency response, and scenario-based training.

Myth 14. *Recruits who fail academy requirements are rarely dismissed.* Reality: Recruits who do not meet standards are routinely separated; failure rates vary but dismissal is common.

Myth 15. *Officers are never disciplined internally for misconduct.* Reality: Departments maintain internal affairs units and disciplinary procedures that can lead to suspension, reassignment, or termination.

Myth 16. *Departments routinely ignore misconduct to protect officers.* Reality: Misconduct investigations follow set procedures; cases are documented, reviewed, and subject to administrative or legal oversight.

Myth 17. *Unions prevent any officer from being fired regardless of conduct.* Reality: Contracts provide due process but do not shield officers from termination when policies or laws are violated.

Myth 18. *Officers freely choose their own work hours and preferred shifts.* Reality: Shift assignments are determined by staffing needs, seniority systems, and operational requirements.

Myth 19. *Every officer works patrol; desk assignments are universal light duty.* Reality: Patrol is common for early careers, but many assignments—detective, training, administrative, specialty units—are standard roles, not light duty.

Myth 20. *Departments cannot adjust staffing levels in response to crime trends.* Reality: Agencies routinely shift personnel, alter deployment, and reassign units based on crime patterns and community needs.

Myth 21. *Police officers receive extra pay whenever they use force.* Reality: Use of force triggers documentation and review, not compensation; officers receive no financial benefit from such incidents.

Appendix M

MOST COMMON POLICE RADIO CODES

10-CODES

10-1: Unable to copy / Signal weak.
10-2: Signal good.
10-4: Acknowledgment / "OK."
10-6: Busy (stand by).
10-7: Out of service.
10-8: In service.
10-9: Repeat message.
10-10: Negative / No.
10-12: Stand by / Unofficial visitors present.
10-13: Advise weather or road conditions.
10-15: En route to station with subject.
10-16: Pick up paperwork.
10-19: Return to station.
10-20: Location.
10-21: Call by phone.
10-22: Cancel / Disregard.
10-23: Arrived at scene.
10-27: Driver's license information.
10-28: Vehicle registration.
10-29: Check for wants or warrants.
10-32: Person with firearm.
10-33: Emergency, all units stand by.
10-36: Correct time.
10-41: Begin tour of duty.
10-42: End tour of duty.
10-50: Traffic crash.
10-51: Tow truck needed.
10-52: Ambulance needed.
10-53: Road blocked.
10-55: Intoxicated driver.
10-56: Intoxicated pedestrian.
10-60: Squad in vicinity.
10-61: Personnel in area.
10-62: Reply by mobile radio.
10-70: Fire alarm.

10-71: Nature of fire.
10-72: Fire progress report.
10-76: En route.
10-78: Need assistance.
10-79: Notify coroner.
10-80: Pursuit in progress.
10-88: Advise telephone number.
10-97: Arrived at assigned location.
10-98: Assignment completed.
10-99: Wanted/stolen indicated.

11-CODES

11-10: Take report.
11-26: Detaining subject / Verification needed.
11-27: Driver's license info, no wants.
11-28: Vehicle registration, no wants.
11-41: Ambulance requested.
11-44: Deceased person.
11-48: Furnish transportation.
11-51: Frequency check.
11-55: Hazardous area.
11-79: Major injury collision.
11-80: Fatal collision.
11-81: Minor injury collision.
11-82: Non-injury collision.
11-83: No details / unknown injuries.
11-99: Officer needs help, emergency.

"SIGNAL CODES"

Signal 1: Officer needs help (emergency).
Signal 3: Hit-and-run crash.
Signal 4: Traffic crash.
Signal 5: Murder.
Signal 7: Dead person.
Signal 8: Missing person.
Signal 9: Stolen tag/plate.
Signal 12: Intoxicated person.
Signal 13: Suspicious person.
Signal 20: Mentally disturbed person.
Signal 21: Burglary.
Signal 22: Disturbance.
Signal 25: Fire.
Signal 27: Prowler.

Signal 28: Robbery.
Signal 29: Reckless driver.
Signal 30: Bomb threat.
Signal 33: Emergency radio traffic only.
Signal 34: Sexual offense.
Signal 37: Juvenile problem.
Signal 41: Stolen vehicle.
Signal 43: Overdose.
Signal 44: Suicide attempt.
Signal 55: Officer down / injured.

PLAIN-LANGUAGE COMMANDS

"Radio check": Confirm audio.
"Copy": Acknowledged.
"En route": Responding to call.
"On scene": Arrived at location.
"Clear": Finished with call.
"Transporting": Carrying a subject.
"Back in service": Available for calls.
"Hold the air": Emergency; restrict radio traffic.
"Code 3": Emergency response; lights and siren.
"Code 4": All clear; situation under control; no further assistance
    needed.

The radio becomes an officer's lifeline in moments like this, turning a few coded words into coordinated action across the patrol network. This policeman's focus behind the wheel reflects how those signals guide everything that follows—identifying the call, shaping the response, and setting the pace of the pursuit. Illustration copyright © Lochlainn Seabrook.

Appendix N

COMMON POLICE ACRONYMS

APB: All Points Bulletin.
APS: Adult Protective Services.
ATF: Bureau of Alcohol, Tobacco, Firearms and Explosives.
BOLO: Be On the Lookout.
CAD: Computer-Aided Dispatch.
CALEA: Commission on Accreditation for Law Enforcement Agencies.
CFS: Call for Service.
CID: Criminal Investigation Division.
CIT: Crisis Intervention Team.
CMV: Commercial Motor Vehicle.
CP: Command Post.
CPD: Community Policing Division.
CSI: Crime Scene Investigation / Investigator.
CSU: Crime Scene Unit.
DDACTS: Data-Driven Approaches to Crime and Traffic Safety.
DEA: Drug Enforcement Administration.
DHS: Department of Homeland Security.
DNR: Department of Natural Resources (law-enforcement branch).
DOT: Department of Transportation.
DRE: Drug Recognition Expert.
DSU: Detective Services Unit.
DV: Domestic Violence.
EMS: Emergency Medical Services.
ETA: Estimated Time of Arrival.
FBI: Federal Bureau of Investigation.
FIO: Field Interview Officer / Field Interview Observation.
FLETC: Federal Law Enforcement Training Centers.
FTO: Field Training Officer.
GOA: Gone on Arrival.
ICE: Immigration and Customs Enforcement.
IDC: Initial Detention Checklist / Inmate Data Card (agency dependent).
IHP: Immediate Hazard to Public.
K9: Police dog unit.

LEA: Law Enforcement Agency.
LEO: Law Enforcement Officer.
LOS: Level of Service / Line of Sight (traffic/crash terminology).
MVA: Motor Vehicle Accident.
NCIC: National Crime Information Center.
NFA: No Further Action / No Further Assistance.
NIBIN: National Integrated Ballistic Information Network.
NIMS: National Incident Management System.
NTA: Notice to Appear (citation in lieu of arrest).
OC: *Oleoresin Capsicum* (pepper spray).
OIS: Officer-Involved Shooting.
PC: Probable Cause.
PD: Police Department / Property Damage (context dependent).
PIO: Public Information Officer.
PPE: Personal Protective Equipment.
PSA: Public Safety Announcement / Public Safety Area.
RMS: Records Management System.
ROW: Right of Way.
SAR: Search and Rescue / Suspicious Activity Report.
SART: Sexual Assault Response Team.
SOP: Standard Operating Procedure.
SRO: School Resource Officer.
SWAT: Special Weapons and Tactics.
TAC: Tactical Channel / Tactical Unit.
TAH: Traffic Accident – Hit.
TAP: Traffic Accident – Property Damage.
TSA: Transportation Security Administration.
UCR: Uniform Crime Reporting.
UI: Unidentified Individual.
VIN: Vehicle Identification Number.
VOI: Vehicle of Interest.
WMD: Weapons of Mass Destruction.
YTD: Year to Date.

Appendix O

APCO RADIOTELEPHONY SPELLING ALPHABET

The APCO (Association of Public-Safety Communications Officials) Radiotelephony Spelling Alphabet is used by many law-enforcement and public-safety agencies to spell names, addresses, license plates, and other important details over the radio. It provides a standardized set of words for each letter, reducing mistakes when similar-sounding letters are spoken in fast, busy, or noisy conditions.

Knowing this alphabet is not required of citizens, but recognizing it can make an encounter smoother. It helps you follow what an officer is spelling, confirm that your information is being transmitted accurately, and provide your own spelling more clearly when asked during a stop, report, or interview.

Because misheard letters can lead to delays, errors, or repeated questions, even basic familiarity with the APCO alphabet gives citizens a simple, practical tool for improving clarity and communication during police encounters.

Developed in the mid-20th Century for police radio use, the APCO system predates today's NATO alphabet and remains in service because many departments still rely on its familiar word set. For citizens, understanding both alphabets simply increases communication confidence in any law-enforcement setting.

A: Adam	N: Nora
B: Boy	O: Ocean
C: Charles	P: Paul
D: David	Q: Queen
E: Edward	R: Robert
F: Frank	S: Sam
G: George	T: Tom
H: Henry	U: Union
I: Ida	V: Victor
J: John	W: William
K: King	X: X-ray
L: Lincoln	Y: Young
M: Mary	Z: Zebra

Analysts in a police crime lab work within strict protocols that determine how evidence is classified, tested, and admitted in court, underscoring the way scientific procedure anchors every stage of a criminal case. Illustration copyright © Lochlainn Seabrook.

GLOSSARY

Abatement: Court-ordered suspension or reduction of penalties.
Accessory: A person who assists in a crime before or after it occurs.
Accomplice: A person who knowingly participates in a crime.
Acquittal: A formal finding of not guilty.
Administrative Hearing: A non-criminal proceeding before an agency.
Administrative Search: A regulatory search for safety, not criminal investigation.
Admissible Evidence: Evidence allowed in court.
Advisement of Rights: Formal notification of constitutional rights.
Affidavit: A sworn written statement submitted to a judge.
Aggravating Factor: A circumstance increasing potential penalty.
Alias: An alternate or false name.
Allegation: A claim that an individual committed an offense.
Appeal: A request for a higher court to review a decision.
Appearance Notice: Court notice directing attendance at a hearing.
Arraignment: First court appearance where charges are read.
Arrest: Lawful custody restricting freedom of movement.
Arrest Report: Official document describing an arrest.
Arrest Warrant: A court order authorizing arrest.
Articulable: Capable of being clearly stated or explained in words.
Articulable Facts: Specific observations supporting legal conclusions.
Assault: Causing fear of immediate physical harm.
Asset Forfeiture: Legal process to seize property connected to criminal activity.
Bail: Money or conditions ensuring appearance in court.
Bail Bond: Financial guarantee posted for a defendant.
Bail Schedule: Standardized bail amounts for common offenses.
Bench Trial: Trial decided by a judge.
Bench Warrant: Warrant for failure to appear in court.
Beyond a Reasonable Doubt: The highest standard of proof.
Blood Alcohol Concentration (BAC): Measured level of alcohol in blood.
Booking: Processing after arrest.
Booking Number: Identification assigned during booking.
Bodycam: Officer-worn video recording device.
Bond: Money or property pledged to secure a person's appearance in court. If the person fails to appear, the bond may be forfeited.
Bond Hearing: Court hearing determining bail.
Brady Material: Evidence favorable to the defense that must be disclosed.
Brief Detention: Temporary stop based on reasonable suspicion.
Burden of Proof: Duty to prove legal claims or charges.
Case Dismissal: Termination of a case without conviction.
Chain of Custody: Documentation showing evidence handling.
Charge: Formal legal allegation against a person.
Citation: Written order requiring court appearance.

Civil Liability: Legal responsibility for monetary damages.
Civil Rights: Rights protected by the Constitution and federal law.
Color of Law: Action taken under governmental authority.
Command Presence: Officer's visible authority.
Community Caretaking: Non-criminal duties performed for public safety.
Complaint: Formal written statement charging an offense.
Compliance: Following lawful police commands.
Concurrent Sentence: Multiple sentences served simultaneously.
Conditional Release: Release subject to specific conditions.
Confession: Voluntary admission of guilt.
Consent: Voluntary and informed agreement.
Consent Search: Search authorized by voluntary permission.
Contact Officer: The officer who speaks directly with the driver or
     pedestrian during a stop, asks questions, and handles identification. This
     role exists only when two or more officers are present, paired with a
     cover officer.
Contempt of Court: Disobedience of a court order.
Contraband: Items illegal to possess.
Conviction: Formal finding of guilt.
Court-Appointed Counsel: Attorney provided to indigent defendants.
Court Date: Scheduled hearing time.
Court Order: Directive issued by a judge.
Crime Scene: Location where an offense occurred.
Criminal Complaint: Document formally charging an offense.
Criminal History: Record of past arrests and convictions.
Criminal Summons: Order directing a person to appear for charges.
Criminal Trespass: Entering property without legal permission or remaining
     after permission has been revoked.
Cross-Examination: Questioning by the opposing side.
Custodial Interrogation: Questioning during custody requiring Miranda
     warnings.
Custody: Circumstances where a person is not free to leave.
Dashcam: Camera mounted in law enforcement vehicles.
Deadly Force: Force likely to cause death or serious injury.
Destructive Search: A destructive search is a police search that damages,
     breaks, or permanently alters property during the course of searching
     for evidence, going beyond what is reasonably necessary to conduct the
     search.
Detainer: Request to hold an individual for another agency.
Detention: Temporary stop for investigation.
Digital Evidence: Electronic data relevant to a case.
Discovery: Exchange of evidence between prosecution and defense.
Discretion: Officer judgment in applying law.
Dismissal: Termination of charges.
Dispatch: Communications center directing officers.
Diversion Program: Alternative program avoiding criminal conviction.
Domestic Incident: Conflict among household or intimate partners.
Due Process: Constitutional guarantee of fair procedures.
Enhancement: Increase in potential penalties due to circumstances.

Excessive Force: Force beyond what is reasonably necessary.
Exculpatory Evidence: Evidence favorable to the defense.
Exigent Circumstances: Emergency allowing warrantless action.
Failure to Appear: Not appearing at scheduled court proceedings.
False Identification: Providing a name or ID not belonging to oneself.
Field Interview (FI): Voluntary questioning without detention.
Field Notes: Observations recorded by officers on scene.
Field Sobriety Tests (FSTs): Physical tests assessing impairment.
Felony: Serious crime punishable by a potential sentence of more than one
    year in prison.
Fifth Amendment: Protection against self-incrimination.
Forensic Evidence: Scientific evidence.
Frisk: Limited pat-down for weapons.
Good Faith: Honest belief that conduct is lawful.
Grand Jury: Panel deciding whether felony charges proceed.
Habeas Corpus: Petition challenging unlawful custody.
Harassment: Behavior intended to annoy or alarm.
Hearsay: Secondhand statements generally inadmissible.
Immunity: Protection from prosecution.
Impeachment (Witness): Challenging credibility of testimony.
Implied Consent: Legal requirement to submit to chemical testing in DUI
    cases.
Inadmissible Evidence: Evidence not permitted in court.
Incident Command System: Structure for emergency response.
Incident Report: Official account of an incident.
Indictment: Formal felony charge issued by a grand jury.
Infraction: Minor violation punishable by fines (e.g., basic speeding).
Initial Appearance: First court hearing after arrest.
Interference: Behavior that disrupts or complicates an officer's duties, even
    without intent to obstruct. It can include failing to follow safety
    instructions or actions that create uncertainty during an encounter.
Interrogation: Police questioning designed to elicit information.
Inventory Search: Search documenting property during impound.
Investigatory Stop: Brief detention based on reasonable suspicion.
Jurisdiction: Legal authority of a court or agency.
Knock-and-Talk: A voluntary encounter in which officers knock, identify
    themselves, and request to speak with an occupant without a warrant.
    The occupant may refuse to speak or deny entry, unless officers develop
    independent legal grounds to enter.
Knock-and-Talk: A voluntary encounter in which officers knock, identify
    themselves, and request to speak with the occupant without a warrant.
    The occupant may refuse to talk or deny entry at any time.
Lawful Order: Police instruction with legal authority.
Miranda Warning: Advisement of rights before custodial interrogation.
    (Named after Ernesto Arturo Miranda, the defendant in the landmark
    U.S. Supreme Court case Miranda v. Arizona, decided in 1966.)
Misdemeanor: Offense punishable by fines or up to a year in jail.
Motion: Formal request to the court.
Mugshot: Booking photograph.

No Contest (Nolo Contendere): Plea not admitting guilt but accepting conviction.

No-Knock Warrant: Warrant allowing unannounced entry.

Nolle Prosequi: A Latin term meaning "we shall no longer prosecute." A prosecutor's formal decision to stop pursuing a criminal charge. It is not a finding of innocence; it simply means the government has chosen not to go forward with the case.

Notice to Appear: Citation requiring court appearance.

Obstruction: Knowingly or intentionally hindering an officer's lawful duties. This is a criminal offense and includes acts such as providing false information, resisting commands, or physically blocking an officer.

Officer Safety: Measures taken for protection during encounters.

Parole: Supervised release after prison.

Passenger Detention: Lawful holding of passengers during a stop.

Pat-Down: Frisk limited to outer clothing.

Perjury: Lying under oath.

Plea: Formal response to charges.

Plea Agreement: Negotiated resolution of a case.

Police Report: Official written account of an incident.

Portable Breath Test (PBT): Handheld breath alcohol test.

Possession: Actual or constructive control over property.

PPE: Protective equipment.

Preliminary Hearing: Hearing to establish probable cause.

Preponderance of Evidence: Civil standard of proof.

Pretext Stop: Traffic stop based on an observed violation despite other suspicion.

Primary Officer: The officer who initiates the stop, directs the encounter, and makes the main investigative and enforcement decisions. This role exists in every stop, regardless of how many officers are present.

Probable Cause: Reasonable belief a crime occurred.

Probation: Court-ordered supervision instead of incarceration.

Processing: Steps taken to log and record an arrested person.

Protective Custody: Temporary detention for safety reasons.

Protective Sweep: Quick check for threats during an arrest.

Proximate Cause: Direct link between action and result.

Reasonable Person Standard: Objective measure of what a typical person would believe.

Reasonable Suspicion: Specific facts supporting a brief detention.

Recognizance: A written promise to appear in court rather than paying bail, based on the person's agreement to return and follow all court conditions.

Record of Arrest: Record documenting arrest activity.

Recusal: Withdrawal of a judge or officer due to conflict.

Resisting: Refusing lawful commands through action.

Restitution: Compensation paid to victims.

Revocation: Cancellation of probation or parole.

Search: Government intrusion where privacy is expected.

Search Incident to Arrest: Search conducted after lawful arrest.

Search Warrant: Judicial permission to search.

Seizure (Person): Restriction of freedom by police.
Seizure (Property): Taking property for evidence or impound.
Sentencing Hearing: Court proceeding determining penalties.
Show of Authority: Officer's actions compelling compliance.
Sobriety Checkpoint: Regulated stop to screen for impaired drivers.
Standing: Legal right to challenge a search or seizure.
Stop: Brief detention for investigation.
Stop-and-Frisk: Stop combined with a frisk for weapons.
Subpoena: Court order requiring appearance or evidence.
Summons: Written notice directing appearance in court.
Supervised Release: Federal post-prison monitoring.
Surety Bond: Bond backed by a third party.
Suspension (License): Temporary loss of driving privileges.
Terry Stop: Investigatory detention based on reasonable suspicion. (Named after John W. Terry, the defendant in the 1968 U.S. Supreme Court case Terry v. Ohio.)
Testimony: Statement under oath.
Tort: A civil wrong that creates legal liability without involving criminal charges; e.g., trespassing, negligence, defamation, nuisance, or battery.
Traffic Infraction: Minor traffic violation.
Trespass: Being on property without the owner's permission.
Trespassing: Entering property without permission, or remaining after being told to leave.
Trial: Formal court proceeding determining guilt.
Use of Force: Physical force used lawfully by police.
Vehicle Impound: Seizure and storage of a vehicle.
Venue: Geographic location of court proceedings.
Verbal Warning: Warning issued without citation.
Voir Dire: Jury selection process.
Want: A law-enforcement alert indicating a person is of interest to an agency but does not involve an active arrest warrant.
Warrant: Judicial authorization for arrest or search.
Warrantless Search: Search under a recognized exception.
Witness Statement: Recorded account given to authorities.
Witness Tampering: Attempt to improperly influence a witness.
Writ: Court-issued order directing action.
Youthful Offender Status: Special designation allowing leniency for young defendants.
Y-Search: A search area focusing on waistband, pockets, and midsection where weapons are commonly hidden.
Zero-Tolerance Policy: Policy requiring action for specific offenses with no discretionary leeway.

High-risk encounters illustrate the narrow margin in which officers must balance threat assessment, lawful force options, and public safety responsibilities under rapidly evolving conditions. In this scenario a K9 officer supports his team's coordinated effort to maintain control while adhering to legal and procedural limits on force. Illustration copyright © Lochlainn Seabrook.

BIBLIOGRAPHY

and Suggested Reading

Blackstone, William. *Commentaries on the Laws of England*. Oxford, UK: Clarendon Press, 1765–1769.

Federal Law Enforcement Training Center. *Constitutional Law Handbook*. Glynco, GA: U.S. Department of Homeland Security, earliest edition available.

LaFave, Wayne R. *Search and Seizure: A Treatise on the Fourth Amendment*. St. Paul, MN: West Publishing, 1978.

Samaha, Joel. *Criminal Procedure*. Belmont, CA: Wadsworth Publishing, 1971.

Seabrook, Lochlainn. *The Constitution of the Confederate States of America Explained: A Clause-by-Clause Study of the South's Magna Carta*. Spring Hill, TN: Sea Raven Press, 2012 Sesquicentennial Civil War Edition.

——. *The Articles of Confederation Explained: A Clause-by-Clause Study of America's First Constitution*. Spring Hill, TN: Sea Raven Press, 2014.

——. *Confederacy 101: Amazing Facts You Never Knew About America's Oldest Political Tradition*. Spring Hill, TN: Sea Raven Press, 2015.

——. *America's Three Constitutions: Complete Texts of the Articles of Confederation, Constitution of the United States of America, and Constitution of the Confederate States of America*. Spring Hill, TN: Sea Raven Press, 2021.

Terry, Charles. *Police Powers and Citizens' Rights*. Chicago, IL: Aldine Publishing, 1969.

United States Congress. *The Constitution of the United States of America*. Washington, D.C.: U.S. Government Printing Office, earliest available edition.

United States Congress. *The Bill of Rights*. Washington, D.C.: U.S. Government Printing Office, earliest available edition.

United States Department of Justice. *Law Enforcement Officers Safety Act Guidelines*. Washington, D.C.: U.S. Government Printing Office, earliest available edition.

United States Department of Justice, National Institute of Justice. *Police Encounters: A National Assessment*. Washington, D.C.: National Institute of Justice, earliest available edition.

United States Department of Justice. *Police Encounters: Constitutional Limits*. Washington, D.C.: U.S. Department of Justice, earliest available edition.

United States Department of Justice. *Understanding Police Use of Force*. Washington, D.C.: U.S. Department of Justice, earliest available edition.

United States Government Publishing Office. *United States Reports*. Washington, D.C.: U.S. Government Printing Office, earliest available volumes.

SUPREME COURT CASES

Alabama v. White, 496 U.S. 325 (1990).
Arizona v. Gant, 556 U.S. 332 (2009).
Arizona v. Johnson, 555 U.S. 323 (2009).
Atwater v. City of Lago Vista, 532 U.S. 318 (2001).
Batson v. Kentucky, 476 U.S. 79 (1986).
Beck v. Ohio, 379 U.S. 89 (1964).
Berger v. New York, 388 U.S. 41 (1967).
Berghuis v. Thompkins, 560 U.S. 370 (2010).
Brendlin v. California, 551 U.S. 249 (2007).
Brinegar v. United States, 338 U.S. 160 (1949).
Bruton v. United States, 391 U.S. 123 (1968).
Cady v. Dombrowski, 413 U.S. 433 (1973).
California v. Acevedo, 500 U.S. 565 (1991).
California v. Carney, 471 U.S. 386 (1985).
Chimel v. California, 395 U.S. 752 (1969).
City of Houston v. Hill, 482 U.S. 451 (1987).
City of Indianapolis v. Edmond, 531 U.S. 32 (2000).
Colorado v. Connelly, 479 U.S. 157 (1986).
Colorado v. Spring, 479 U.S. 564 (1987).
Davis v. United States, 512 U.S. 452 (1994).
Dunaway v. New York, 442 U.S. 200 (1979).
Florida v. Bostick, 501 U.S. 429 (1991).
Florida v. Jardines, 569 U.S. 1 (2013).
Georgia v. Randolph, 547 U.S. 103 (2006).
Graham v. Connor, 490 U.S. 386 (1989).
Hiibel v. Sixth Judicial District Court, 542 U.S. 177 (2004).
Illinois v. Caballes, 543 U.S. 405 (2005).
Illinois v. Gates, 462 U.S. 213 (1983).
Illinois v. Lafayette, 462 U.S. 640 (1983).
Illinois v. McArthur, 531 U.S. 326 (2001).
Illinois v. Wardlow, 528 U.S. 119 (2000).
J.L. v. Florida, 529 U.S. 266 (2000).
Johnson v. United States, 333 U.S. 10 (1948).
Katz v. United States, 389 U.S. 347 (1967).
Kyllo v. United States, 533 U.S. 27 (2001).
Mapp v. Ohio, 367 U.S. 643 (1961).
Maryland v. Buie, 494 U.S. 325 (1990).
Maryland v. King, 569 U.S. 435 (2013).
Michigan v. Long, 463 U.S. 1032 (1983).
Minnesota v. Carter, 525 U.S. 83 (1998).
Minnesota v. Dickerson, 508 U.S. 366 (1993).
Minnesota v. Olson, 495 U.S. 91 (1990).
Miranda v. Arizona, 384 U.S. 436 (1966).
Missouri v. McNeely, 569 U.S. 141 (2013).
New York v. Belton, 453 U.S. 454 (1981).
Payton v. New York, 445 U.S. 573 (1980).

Pennsylvania v. Mimms, 434 U.S. 106 (1977).
Riley v. California, 573 U.S. 373 (2014).
Robinson v. United States, 414 U.S. 218 (1973).
Rodriguez v. United States, 575 U.S. 348 (2015).
Safford Unified School District v. Redding, 557 U.S. 364 (2009).
Schneckloth v. Bustamonte, 412 U.S. 218 (1973).
Sharpe v. United States, 470 U.S. 675 (1985).
Stewart v. United States, 486 U.S. 128 (1988).
Tennessee v. Garner, 471 U.S. 1 (1985).
Terry v. Ohio, 392 U.S. 1 (1968).
United States v. Chadwick, 433 U.S. 1 (1977).
United States v. Drayton, 536 U.S. 194 (2002).
United States v. Jones, 565 U.S. 400 (2012).
United States v. Matlock, 415 U.S. 164 (1974).
United States v. Mendenhall, 446 U.S. 544 (1980).
United States v. Robinson, 414 U.S. 218 (1973).
United States v. Ross, 456 U.S. 798 (1982).
United States v. Sokolow, 490 U.S. 1 (1989).
Warden v. Hayden, 387 U.S. 294 (1967).
Whren v. United States, 517 U.S. 806 (1996).
Wong Sun v. United States, 371 U.S. 471 (1963).

CONSTITUTIONAL TEXTS

United States Congress. *The Bill of Rights*. Washington, D.C.: U.S. Government Printing Office, earliest available edition.
United States Congress. *The Constitution of the United States of America*. Washington, D.C.: U.S. Government Printing Office, earliest available edition.

Routine foot patrols often reflect the most visible side of local law enforcement, where casual interactions and steady presence help develop and maintain public trust. Illustration copyright © Lochlainn Seabrook.

INDEX

burglary, 97, 99, 100, 103, 110
burglary of a vehicle, 100
CAD, 113
CALEA, 113
California v. Acevedo, 80, 124
call for service, 113
camera, 42, 118
canine units, 81
carjacking, 100
Carroll v. United States, 77
carrying a concealed weapon illegally, 100
cars, 33, 62
case dismissal, 117
case law, 8, 9, 62, 63, 66
cemeteries, 100
center console, 34
CFS, 113
chain of custody, 117
charge, 52, 92, 93, 97, 117, 119, 120
charges, 7, 14, 18, 27, 49-52, 58, 66, 91, 92, 95-97, 117-121
check fraud, 100
child abuse, 100
child endangerment, 100
child exploitation, 97, 100
child molestation, 100
child neglect, 100
Chimel v. California, 78, 124
CID, 113
CIT, 113
citation, 30, 58, 73, 74, 106, 107, 114, 118, 120, 121
citation activity, 107
citations, 89, 105, 107
citizen obligations, 73, 74
citizen rights, 47, 66, 82
citizens, 5, 6, 8-10, 13-15, 17-19, 21, 22, 27, 29, 31, 47, 57, 59, 62, 63, 65-68, 73, 78, 79, 82-88, 90, 93, 97, 105, 106, 115, 150, 151
City of Houston v. Hill, 83, 124
civil liability, 118
civil rights, 90, 118
clarity, 8, 10, 13, 17, 21, 27, 35, 51, 54, 55, 66, 67, 74, 75, 86, 88, 91, 93, 115
Class A, 91
Class B, 91

Class C, 91
Class D, 91
class system, 91
classes, 89, 90
clear, 15, 17, 21, 25-27, 29, 31, 33, 42, 43, 46, 47, 49, 53, 55, 56, 59, 63, 65-68, 74, 75, 78, 79, 81, 84-88, 93, 106, 111, 150
clothing, 22, 120
CMV, 113
collateral consequences, 90, 91
color of law, 100, 118
command post, 113
command presence, 118
commands, 15, 23, 43, 47, 54, 58, 66, 67, 82, 84, 87, 101, 111, 118, 120
commercial burglary, 100
commercial motor vehicle, 113
commission on accreditation for law enforcement agencies, 113
common crimes, 7, 99
communication, 13, 15, 19, 23, 26, 39, 43, 47, 51, 53-56, 59, 63, 66, 67, 76, 88, 104, 106, 115
community caretaking, 118
community policing division, 113
community service, 89, 96
compartments, 27, 34, 35, 87, 88
compensation, 107, 108, 120
complaint, 118
compliance, 28, 75, 76, 106, 118, 121
computer-aided dispatch, 113
computer checks, 23
computer intrusion, 100
concealing identity, 100
concurrent sentence, 118
conditional release, 118
conditional sentences, 91, 93
conduct, 13, 14, 17, 18, 21, 23-27, 34, 35, 37, 41, 43, 49, 51, 53, 54, 57, 59, 79, 83, 84, 87, 89-92, 97, 100-103, 107, 108, 118, 119
confession, 47, 118
confusion, 9, 10, 13, 21, 25, 27, 54, 59, 86, 87

dating violence, 100
DDACTS, 113
DEA, 95, 113
deadly force, 79, 118
defacing property, 100, 104
defamation, 121
defendants, 85, 89, 93, 118, 121
defiance, 67
defrauding an innkeeper, 100
Degree system, 91
Delaware v. Prouse, 78
Department of Homeland
    Security, 113, 123
Department of Natural Resources,
    113
Department of Transportation,
    113
department policy, 34, 107
departmental procedure, 66
deprivation of rights under color
    of law, 100
desecration, 99, 100
destination, 73
destructive search, 34, 118
detainee's rights, 63
detainer, 118
detective services unit, 113
detectives, 95
detention, 18, 22, 23, 26, 28, 30,
    31, 35, 39, 45, 50, 54, 58,
    62, 63, 66, 74-76, 84, 91,
    113, 117 121
detention facility, 50
detentions, 21, 23, 24, 54, 63, 66,
    77, 79, 82
DHS, 113
digital evidence, 118
disagreement, 59, 84
disarming a peace officer, 101
disciplinary procedures, 108
discovery, 34, 118
discretion, 8, 9, 19, 34, 118
dismissal, 108, 117, 118
disorderly conduct, 101
dispatch, 106, 113, 118
distribution, 101
disturbing the peace, 101
diversion, 89, 92, 118
diversion program, 118
diversion programs, 89
DNR, 113

documentation, 14, 22, 63, 107,
    108, 117
documentation quality, 107
domestic battery, 101
domestic incident, 118
domestic violence, 97, 101, 113
DOT, 113
DRE, 113
driver, 18, 29, 31, 59, 73, 75, 76,
    78, 80, 88, 105, 106, 109,
    111, 118
driver behavior, 29
driver's license, 22, 30, 57, 73,
    74, 105, 109, 110
driveway, 38
driving, 105
driving privileges, 90, 121
driving violation, 35
drug enforcement administration,
    113
drug manufacturing, 101
drug paraphernalia possession, 101
drug possession, 97, 101
drug recognition expert, 113
drug trafficking, 97, 101
drug trafficking across state lines,
    97
drug-sniffing dog, 81
DSU, 113
due process, 50, 51, 63, 108, 119
DUI, 80, 89, 90, 97, 99, 101, 119
DUI education, 89
DUI-related cases, 90
duties, 13, 26, 41, 43, 47, 53, 58,
    59, 61, 62, 65, 66, 72, 74,
    83, 84, 94, 118-120
DV, 113
DWI, 101
eavesdropping, 101
economic harm, 92
elder abuse, 101
elected district attorneys, 96
embezzlement, 101
emergency, 29, 37, 38, 40, 76,
    92, 108-111, 113, 119
emergency lights, 29
emergency medical services, 113
emergency responders, 92
employment, 90
EMS, 113
encounter, 4, 9, 10, 13-15, 17-19,

public safety area, 114
public-policy concerns, 93
pullover, 28
punishment, 51, 76, 92, 93
pursuit, 38, 101, 110, 112
questioning, 19, 21, 23, 27, 35,
    45-48, 50, 54, 55, 66, 74,
    77-79, 86, 118, 119
questions, 14, 18, 21-23, 25, 27,
    30, 33, 37, 39, 41, 45-47,
    49-51, 53, 54, 57, 73, 74, 85,
    86, 106, 115, 118
quotas, 107
radio, 7, 106, 109, 111, 112, 115
rape, 103
rapid response, 97
reasonable force, 27, 51, 75, 76
reasonable person standard, 120
reasonable suspicion, 10, 14, 18,
    19, 21-23, 26, 30, 31, 34, 35,
    49, 54, 62, 66, 73, 74, 78,
    81, 82, 117, 119-121
receiving stolen property, 103
reckless driving, 103, 104
reckless endangerment, 103
recognizance, 50, 120
record of arrest, 120
recording, 7, 23, 26, 39, 41-43,
    50, 59, 84, 101, 104, 117
recording police , 26
recordings, 42
records, 55, 63, 114
records management system, 114
recusal, 120
refusal, 18, 23, 26, 33, 35, 57, 73,
    74, 87, 88, 105, 106
regulatory breaches, 89
release, 23, 47, 50, 76, 96, 118,
    120, 121
remedial courses, 89
removal, 7, 31, 75, 76
required items, 57
resistance, 27, 47, 55, 76
resisting, 103, 106, 120
resisting arrest, 103
respect, 10, 17, 66, 68, 76, 82,
    88, 150, 151
responsibilities, 58, 65-67, 72,
    121, 150
restitution, 89, 90, 96, 120
restitution requirements, 96

restraints, 51
restricted zones, 42
restrictions, 42, 43, 90
retail fraud, 103
retaliation, 42, 76
revenue generation, 107
revocation, 121
Rhode Island v. Innis, 78
right of way, 114
rights, 4, 7-10, 13-15, 17, 22,
    25-29, 31, 33, 35, 39, 41, 43,
    45-48, 50, 51, 53, 55, 57, 59,
    62, 63, 65-67, 74, 77, 82, 84,
    86-88, 90, 100, 106,
    117-119, 123, 125, 150
risk, 14, 15, 23, 26, 35, 38, 42,
    51, 53, 54, 62, 65, 76, 84,
    86, 87, 89, 91-93, 102, 121
RMS, 114
roadside, 18, 54, 60, 67, 75, 76,
    78, 79, 82, 88
robbery, 97, 99, 103, 111
Rodriguez v. United States, 81,
    82, 125
Roosevelt, Theodore, 9
routine stops, 19, 53
ROW, 114
rulings, 14, 73, 82
sabotage, 103
sacred items, 100
safety, 9, 10, 13-15, 17-19,
    22-24, 26, 29, 31-35, 38, 39,
    41-43, 45-47, 49-51, 53-56,
    58, 59, 62, 66, 67, 72-84, 89,
    92, 97, 103, 108, 113-115,
    117-121, 123
safety-based commands, 58, 66
safety checks, 24, 31, 55
safety classes, 89
safety concerns, 23, 35, 43, 53,
    58, 75, 78, 80
safety measures, 23, 53, 77, 82
Salinas v. Texas, 85
sanctions, 89, 90
SAR, 114
SART, 114
scenario-based training, 108
Schneckloth v. Bustamonte, 78,
    81, 125
school resource officer, 114
Sea Raven Press, 152

statutory maximum, 91
statutory rape, 103
steering wheel, 29, 32
stop, 7, 9, 13-15, 17-19, 21-23,
    25-27, 29-31, 33, 35, 41-43,
    45-47, 50, 54, 55, 57-60, 62,
    65, 66, 71, 73-84, 88, 101,
    102, 105, 106, 115, 117-121
stop-and-frisk, 121
stop-and-identify, 22
stop-and-identify states, 73
stops, 7, 13, 18, 19, 21, 22, 28,
    29, 37, 42, 45, 49, 53-55, 58,
    62, 63, 66, 73, 74, 78-82,
    105, 106
subpoena, 121
summons, 118, 121
supervised release, 120, 121
supervisory approval, 107
Supreme Court, 7, 20, 73, 77, 83,
    87, 96, 119, 121, 124
Supreme Court cases, 7, 77, 124
surety bond, 121
suspect, 38, 79, 85
suspended sentences, 92
suspension (license), 121
suspicion, 10, 14, 18, 19, 21-23,
    26, 30, 31, 34, 35, 49, 54,
    55, 62, 66, 67, 73-75, 78, 81,
    82, 87, 117, 119-121
suspicious activity report, 114
SWAT, 114
TAC, 114
tactical channel, 114
tactical unit, 114
TAH, 114
TAP, 114
task forces, 95
tax evasion, 103
temporary stops, 49
Tennessee v. Garner, 79, 125
tension, 14, 15, 19, 29-31, 53,
    65, 67, 75
terrorism (state-level), 103
Terry Rule, 18, 19
Terry Stop, 77, 121
Terry v. Ohio, 14, 18, 54, 77,
    121, 125
Terry, John W., 121
testimony, 119, 121
theft, 34, 92, 97, 99, 101-103

theft by deception, 103
theft by receiving, 103
Third Degree, 92
threat, 23, 59, 79, 92, 99, 103,
    106, 111, 121
threatening a public official, 103
threats to life, 38
tort, 121
traffic citations, 89
traffic enforcement, 19, 62
traffic infraction, 121
traffic misdemeanors, 97
traffic school, 89
traffic stop, 7, 14, 26, 29-31, 35,
    45, 57-59, 62, 66, 71, 73-76,
    81, 82, 101, 105, 120
traffic stops, 7, 22, 29, 54, 55, 62,
    66, 73, 74, 78-81, 106
transport, 50-52
transportation security
    administration, 114
transporting, 101, 102
travelers, 105
traveling, 105
treatment programs, 90, 96
trespass, 100, 118, 121
trespassing, 121
trial, 117, 121
trunk, 34
TSA, 114
U.S. District Court, 96
U.S. Marshals, 95
U.S. Secret Service, 95
UCR, 114
UI, 114
unauthorized practice of a
    profession, 104
unauthorized use of a vehicle, 104
unclassified offenses, 92
unidentified individual, 114
uniform crime reporting, 114
United States of America, 4, 123,
    125
United States v. Arvizu, 81
United States v. Drayton, 81, 125
United States v. Ross, 79, 125
units, 55, 81, 97, 108, 109
unlawful assembly, 104
unlawful conduct, 53, 89
unlawful entry, 38
unlawful imprisonment, 104

MEET THE AUTHOR

LOCHLAINN SEABROOK is a bestselling American author, award-winning historian, acclaimed artist and filmmaker, and lifelong writer-researcher whose work spans history, religion, law, and science. Known for his clear, accessible writing style, he has written over one hundred evidence-based books that emphasize accuracy, practical knowledge, and the empowerment of everyday citizens.

Drawing on decades of research in constitutional principles, legal history, and real-world police–citizen interactions, Seabrook developed *The Citizen's Guide to Police Encounters* to provide a concise, neutral, and easy-to-understand handbook for all Americans. His goal is to help readers navigate police encounters with confidence, respect, and an informed understanding of their rights and responsibilities.

An avid outdoorsman, Kentucky Colonel, and respected scholar of American constitutional law, he lives and works in the Rocky Mountains, where he continues to produce educational resources designed to strengthen public understanding of American law and civic life.

For more information on Mr. Seabrook visit

LochlainnSeabrook.com

Effective policing rests on steady professionalism, which includes an officer's demeanor. This element plays a central role in establishing lawful order and mutual respect throughout every encounter with citizens. Illustration copyright © Lochlainn Seabrook.

Nurture Your Mind, Body, and Spirit!

READ THE BOOKS OF

SEA RAVEN PRESS

Visit our Webstore for a wide selection of wholesome, family–friendly, evidence–based, educational books for all ages. You'll be glad you did!

Artisan-Crafted Books & Merch From the Rocky Mountains

THANK YOU FOR SUPPORTING OUR SMALL AMERICAN FAMILY BUSINESS!

SeaRavenPress.com

Visit our sister sites:
LochlainnSeabrook.com
YouTube.com/user/SeaRavenPress
YouTube.com/@SeabrookFilms
Rumble.com/user/SeaRavenPress
Pond5.com/artist/LochlainnSeabrook

SEA RAVEN PRESS

Artisan-Crafted Books & Merch From the Rocky Mountains

L.S.

If you enjoyed this book you will be interested in Colonel Seabrook's other popular related titles:

☛ AMERICA'S THREE CONSTITUTIONS:
COMPLETE TEXTS OF THE ARTICLES OF CONFEDERATION, U.S. CONSTITUTION, AND C.S. CONSTITUTION

☛ THE ARTICLES OF CONFEDERATION EXPLAINED:
A CLAUSE-BY-CLAUSE STUDY OF AMERICA'S FIRST CONSTITUTION

Available from Sea Raven Press and wherever fine books are sold.

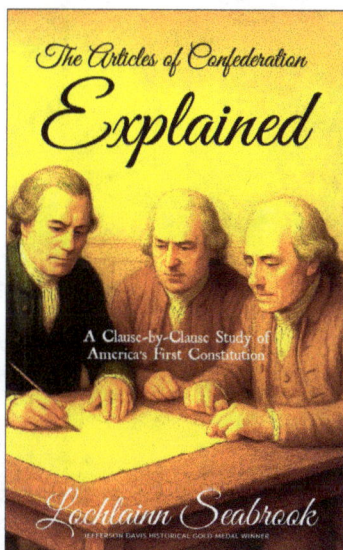

www.ingramcontent.com/pod-product-compliance
Lightning Source LLC
Chambersburg PA
CBHW072154270326
41930CB00011B/2422